M000283836

The
Handbag
of
Happiness

The Handbag of Happiness

And other misunderstandings, misdemeanours and misadventures

ALANNAH HILL

Hardie Grant

BOOKS

Alannah Hill is an iconic designer, bestselling author and sought-after public speaker. For seventeen years she was the creative director of the trailblazing brand she founded, Alannah Hill. In 2015 she left and launched her own label, Louise Love. Alannah's memoir, *Butterfly on a Pin*, was released to critical acclaim in 2018. She lives in Melbourne with her son and her beaglier, Jack.

For my son, Edward.
Our children will always be the sun around
which we spin, long after they've untied our
apron strings. And their baby hands the only
hands of which we can never let go.

And to you, dear reader.
Are you tired of opening a book and not seeing
your name in the dedication? I am too, so
The Handbag of Happiness is also for you!

A letter for you

Welcome to *The Handbag of Happiness, and Other Misunderstandings, Misdemeanours and Misadventures.*

Stop sweeping and mopping and feeling guilty! You've done the right thing in purchasing my book today, so stuff it inside your handbag, kick off your sky-high heels, run yourself a bath, pour yourself a dessert sherry, love, and listen to me!

You've come to understand that life doesn't go according to plan, no matter how perfectly laid out your life plans might have been. You've told yourself you're young at heart and can get through anything. That age is just mind over matter – and if you don't mind, it doesn't matter. You've already guessed that we can't always get what we want and that often we get what we *don't* want *or* need. You might be marvelling at how parenting wouldn't be so difficult if we didn't care how our children turned out, and how in time our little miracles naturally turn away from us, leaving us bereft, resentful, confused and very, very sad!

Life throws jewels and baubles and sometimes a brooch of bad luck our way, making us tick tick ticking little timebombs ready to explode at any given moment.

I'm ready to explode at any given moment!

I explode quite regularly, don't you?

I believed I had no words left in me after I wrote my memoir, *Butterfly on a Pin*. I was bereft of the written word but, unfortunately, I still felt like I was going to explode (at any given moment).

And so I reinvented myself as a public speaker, speaking at events about trauma, resilience, lovelessness, how to become successful, how not to become successful and how not to make the same mistakes I did.

Reinvention can be a tremendous thing, but then I was back to being just me – because we take ourselves wherever we go.

And so, one blistering, hazy Sunday afternoon around 4 pm … I started writing again!

Real-life episodes from my life tumbled onto the page, causing an occasional howl of laughter and the odd sparkly tear, stories about what happens when things don't go according to plan – which, in my experience, is pretty much most of the time!

I wanted to jam-pack *The Handbag of Happiness* with black humour about modern-day chaos, with punked-up defiant stories, like the time I turned a Mentos lolly into a tooth and the tooth flew right out of my mouth (in public!). You'll find that splendidly embarrassing story in 'The Handkerchief of Bravado'.

I wanted to write about lament, love, shame, resilience, triumph, silent sadness, delusion, disdain and utopia with mini-epiphanies, anti-epiphanies and a new kind of epiphany I haven't thought of yet.

I hope my stories bring a gentle, hilarious and devilish, zen-like calmness while you sit reading under your favourite tree …

And I hope to see you soon, just you and misdemeanour me!

love, Hannah

The handbag of
happiness

C an a really, really expensive designer handbag make you happy?

Twelve years ago, I bought a really, *really* expensive handbag because I thought it would make me happy. My Miu Miu handbag dazzled with black and silver Italian sequins, often startling envious bystanders into staring at it until they risked going blind. The interior of the Miu Miu was black kid leather, the clasp innovative and silvery cool. The handbag was so *devastatingly* beautiful that I forked out $4000 for it – the *most* money I have *ever* spent on an accessory, a shoe or a handbag.

I didn't believe in wasting money on designer clothing, jewellery or handbags. I preferred the knock-offs because I always ruin the interior of a bag. Lipstick, hairspray and lip gloss – they all *love* blowing themselves to pieces inside my handbags. I think it's because I leave my bags in the hot sun and it somehow forces the lipstick and hairspray to just kind of ... blow up – lipstick everywhere!

I believed in spending money on designer kitchens, marble bathrooms, vintage hand-blown pink chandeliers, dodgy real estate and a staggering shares portfolio with $300 worth of Rio Tinto and a few diamond shares. (Unfortunately, the Rin Tin Tin soon plummeted to catastrophic new lows and looked like it might never regain consciousness.)

But suddenly I wanted to know what it felt like to say, 'My *bag*? Oh … it's *Miu Miu*!' You see, I was a successful 45-year-old businesswoman but I'd never owned a designer handbag. I didn't think I deserved to and, quite frankly, I thought people who purchased handbags over $1000 were insane! The few people I allowed inside my home would often comment on what they considered a *disappointing*, lacklustre, designer-deprived wardrobe.

'… not *even* a Dolce & Gabbana *wallet*? *Chanel* purse? A Balenciaga *tampon* holder? Come *on* … you *must* have a few vintage Yves Saint Laurent leather totes lying around? They're iconic!'

Yeah … and they're $50K!

One bitter-cold November afternoon when I was in New York for business, I marched into Bergdorf Goodman on Fifth Avenue, slammed the ludicrous $4000 onto my Black American Express card and then levitated.

I'd never been so happy in all my life! In fact, I was so happy I levitated six floors up, suddenly appearing in the fancy Bergdorf Goodman restaurant, where I congratulated myself with a Bergdorf burger and Diet Coke. I'd done it! I finally owned a designer handbag. My handbag suggested to everybody I swanked toward that I was a successful person showing economic prosperity – the stains of childhood insecurity miraculously gone!

For ten minutes I was so puffed up with happiness I felt like a bright red helium balloon.

And then the happiness disappeared. And so did the red helium balloon.

After ten minutes, I was back to being me. Just me in an NYC department store, spending $4000 on a bag in the hope it would make me happy. And it did, but only for ten minutes.

I often ask myself the question, *What does make women happy?*

And the brutal answer is, nothing! Not for more than ten minutes at a time. But perhaps those perfect ten minutes are worth living for, and the hours that circle them worth fighting for, making the ten minutes feel just a little bit longer.

Postscript: I was burgled in 2013. My new Mercedes-Benz was stolen from the garage, three laptops, iPads, four phones, Chanel sunglasses … *all* stolen … along with the happiness glitter bag! I was devastated. Mainly about the happiness bag! I worked alongside a St Kilda detective and helped him track down the bag. I found it on Facebook! The burglar had given my car and happiness bag to his mother, who of course *had* to show off her new stolen gifts online. The mum stood proudly next to my stolen Mercedes clutching my happiness handbag. Her crim son lay spread-eagled across the car bonnet wearing my black Chanel sunglasses with a sanctimonious crim-like smirk.

Mother and son were eventually caught, but the only thing I really wanted was that bag back.

Two weeks later the detective from St Kilda knocked at my front door. He was hand-delivering my Miu Miu happiness bag. I felt the rush of red helium balloon happiness all over again – but only for ten minutes – and then I was back to being just me!

The frock of
how dare you!

I 'm a loner. And if you take the L and R out of loner, there you have it: one.

L one R

Loners like to walk aimlessly because that's what loners do.

It took me years to discover the pleasures of walking aimlessly because you *can't* walk aimlessly when you're strapped into a pair of sky-high heels. It pains me now to think that in my more *immature* years, I thought walking was reserved for those afflicted by singledoom, and isolated co-dependent pessimistic couples. I was very alarmed by walking new mums who hogged the footpaths with great big terrifying prams, but if I saw a dad with a baby in a pram or a toddler in a stroller, I'd smile and wink with a little stroller-by flirting. (I don't know what I wanted but I'm sure it was admirable.) I thought walking was for people with a few extra kilos on the hips, those with a love for the jam donut and an ice-cold beer.

That was until I found the loner in me and hit the streets in vintage Nikes chosen by my son. I soon discovered how light I could feel. My feet were no longer in shoe jail and I found myself taking much bigger walking risks with my new quick steps.

Of an evening, I liked to walk through the streets with Jack the dog and a pair of secateurs, snip-snip-snipping … a rose here, a lemon there, a lavender bush over there … I loved a grand, rundown house amid a grand, rundown garden in a rundown cobbled back street. I loved gardens left to flourish unattended, leaving flowers and citrus fruits *flowing* onto the footpath, meaning they were there *for the taking*.

I called it 'the overhang'.

Mine for the taking!

When I was a high-flying designer, my salary package included a weekly delivery of fresh flowers from legendary Fitzroy florist Flowers Vasette. After I left the company in 2014, the bouquets of freshly cut roses were one of the perks to go. I thought about making a Faustian flower deal with Vasette … but instead chose to rely on the 'overhang'.

I'd carry armfuls of overhang through the doors of my Victorian house. Each room looked like a funeral parlour but I didn't care. The dining room smelt gorgeous and my bedroom was a funeral parlour dream. I snipped oranges, hydrangeas, garden roses and, one time, I accidentally dug up a boronia bush in a rundown apartment block.

I once asked a policeman (after being chastised for carrying armloads of overhang) to please clarify whether overhang was public or private property. The policeman stared right into my eyes and said in long, slow syllables, 'Well, there's no law stating that a person cannot take flowers or citrus fruit from an overhanging branch – no law that I *know of*. But, look, people just don't like it – in fact, they *hate* you for it.'

I carried on with my evening walking. That policeman had no idea what he was talking about.

But what I discovered through my new passion for walking were people living rough on the streets, their sleeping bags scattered across the footpath. I could feel their intolerable sadness all sausaged up inside.

People living rough on the streets have always made me feel terribly sad, curious and guilty all at the same time. What did I do? Not enough. I didn't know what to do. And that's why I felt guilty. Not to mention Jack's scavenging of their KFC – he wolfed it down, even crunching the chicken bones.

D eep down, I think we're all a little alarmed by the homeless. The combination of hopelessness and dispossession is too much for us to take in, and so we look the other way. I try my best not to be judgemental, but I sometimes fail, so I settle for a little bit of judging here, a little bit of judging there and a lot of judging over there – a little bit of judgy Alannah everywhere!

I have a lifelong habit of stickybeaking into every conversation within earshot, which is why I often find myself conducting *60 Minutes*–style interviews with some of the wilder characters.

Sometimes the saddest part about the interviews were that the person they dreamt of becoming was just a breath away, but through bad luck, drugs or truly awful parents, they found themselves living rough on the streets. I'd learnt a lot in my fifty-six years on this earth – I thought nobody could fool me because I wouldn't allow it. I was reinvented and un-foolable! I'd also developed the art of the bird's-eye view, so that in the middle of a little self-generated chaos, I'd float up from myself, metres above the carnage, stare down and think, *Oh dear, look at you, Alannah. Are you really going to soldier on with this idea?* And the 'real' me would think, *Well, I'm in the thick of it now … But I can handle anything – I was, after all, officially Wonder Woman of the Year!*[*]

But sometimes my bird's-eye view held no perspective at all.

One particular evening I was walking past the tram stop, delicately stepping over the rough sleepers around the supermarket entrance. The magic hour had magically disappeared, and the first blast of night sprawled across the midnight skies. I was eating my fourth mini Magnum (and had two more secretly tucked in my pocket).

And then I saw him. A shadow. An outline – barely a person. Limping toward me in black denim jeans with no shoes, no socks, no shirt. He asked for a flower from my overhang and a lemon. Where was his sleeping bag and the KFC for Jack? My FBI eyes scanned his inflamed red skin and sensed his deep longing for someone or something. He was shaking and convulsing; large sections of his torso and back were blistering, while other parts looked like a family of deathly jellyfish had taken up residence. His head was shaved, showing a poorly executed tattoo that simply said 'what' (no question mark). He was stocky, forlorn, despondent and inexplicably angry.

And then I saw it – he had no ears!

As in *ear-less* …

---

[*] It's true! In 2019 I was crowned Momentum Wonder Woman of the Year.

I tried not to stare but I was a long-time stare-bear. I could not look away.

'Flower Lady! Heh! Flower Girl … you're an angel – you're beautiful … I can see right into your eyes … I can see you …'

Don't fall for this, Alannah, I told myself. These kinds of compliments could easily trigger compassion and huge amounts of misplaced sympathy and, to top it off, a momentary loss of judgement. Jack was very much on guard, his beagle nose in overdrive, sniffing murderously. My stickybeak curiosity hit an all-time high. Did he *really* think I was an angel, or was he just in an altered state? I was *all ears!*

My straight-up FBI questions were getting terrific results. He was quite tuned into ears. He told me they had nothing to do with how we hear – he spoke about frequencies and how we only use 10 per cent of our hearing. He thought ears were pointless!

'Ya eardrums are like … nowhere near ya ears, so ya don't even need ears!'

'So … we don't need ears but … where are *your* ears?'

He told me they had been bludgeoned off by a cellmate during a long stint in jail for a crime he didn't commit. He'd traded his ears for a gram of meth.

'What did the person do with your cut-off ears? Who'd even want a pair of ears?'

'Who *wouldn't* want a pair of ears in jail, darlin'? Jesus, you know nuthin' … ya protected if you can get ears – king of the whole jail … ya can get anything ya want from the screws. Fuck, darlin', haven'tcha ever been in jail?'

'The pain though? How did you handle the pain?'

'It was nuthin' – like getting a good clip round the ears,' he said grimly, not even aware he'd made a little joke.

No Ears looked sixty-five but was only twenty-three. And once I started with my curious questions, nothing could stop him talking. He told me he'd been in jail half his life, that he knew he was a 'fuck-up', but he wanted to see his parents. They'd closed the shutters on parenting and were ignoring his overtures. He said all he'd done was to steal his parents' three cars, the family caravan and their priceless family heirlooms. He'd once hacked their bank accounts, but he got caught. He didn't understand why his parents had taken out a restraining order and why they wouldn't forgive him.

I wanted to tell No Ears the sad, unholy truth. Drugs and alcohol were not his problem: his reality was. He hadn't felt a molecule of love for himself or from anybody else for years. He was lonely. Afraid. Complicated. A drug addict. Addiction starts with pain and ends with pain. It was impossible for me to imagine No Ears as an innocent newborn with a mother who loved him.

I felt a rush of sympathy and gave him a lemon from the overhang and my spare mini Magnum ice-creams – a kind of love, I told him, even if they had melted.

The next morning, decked out in a brand-new frock and matching runners, I was fast-stepping it home from my son Ed's school run and, to be honest, I thought I'd never looked better. The dress was made from 100 per cent silk with 100 per cent silk lining, and was covered in vintage red roses. It was a glamorous Alannahfied version of a 'housecoat' and was perfect for walking. It was loose where it needed to be and firm where it needed to be. (I attempted to design matching Spanx but they weren't so triumphant.) The sleeves were bell-shaped and, because I loved a pocket, the frock featured a French envelope–style pocket, lined in red silk, precisely cut to hold a pair of ladies' gardening secateurs. I mean, who knows when I'd be required to do a spot of public pruning?

This particular morning, as I approached my house I saw the boot of my Batmobile was wide open. That was odd. I'd never leave the boot open. Had I left my keys inside?

I walked around to the driver's side and instinctively baulked – there was a strange man in the driver's seat.

It was No Ears.

I couldn't hear my heart beat or feel my legs.

No Ears had followed me home, No Ears had waited for me to slip out and now No Ears was *in my car*.

How. Dare. You.

I quickly turned into a trifecta of the Hulk, Wonder Woman and a rabies-riddled German shepherd, showing no fear. I barked ferociously and saw his arms flailing through the air, his face a black hole as he ripped the rear-vision mirror off and stabbed the sound system with a knife. No Ears had no mercy. He was literally tearing my car apart.

I couldn't believe I'd shared my ice-cream with him. I turned into Lucifer when I saw my handbag of happiness being thrown around the car. I was suddenly the fourth member of a punked-up Charlie's Angels team.

'GET OUT OF MY EFFING CAR,' I yelled at him. 'You're not going to find redemption *there*!'

'This is myyyyyyyy CAAAAR – you stole it – you're the devil,' he shouted back through the window. 'You're NOT even here. Are you a fucking cop? You're a COP, aren'tcha?'

I stopped shrieking and backed away, my eyes drilling into him. I concentrated on pregnant pauses for maximum effect: 'Just. Get. Out. Of. My. Car.'

Silence … and then No Ears reanimated.

'WHERE'S the keys? I got a job interview in Adelaide at midnight then I'm drivin' TO AYERS FUCKING ROCK! STOP asking questions! I told that Nazi doctor and all of youse that I'm not doin' it no more. I'm not taking ya pills for any mental illness cos ya know what – I figured it out. I'm not mental – YOUSE all are!'

'I'll give you ten seconds,' I warned. 'I have a weapon in my pocket and I'm not afraid to use it.'

I counted back from ten …

And then No Ears opened the door and jumped out.

He pushed past me with a giant kick to my shins. I refused to let him see me double over in pain. He ran to the front of the car and stood there with his arms crossed, shouting about how he was going to cut my ears off if I called the police. In my head, I sharpened my blades and reloaded my guns. *I'll fight him with any weapon, even my lady secateurs.*

On high alert and wondering what I might have left on the car console, I ordered him to empty his pockets. For a moment I saw the frightened little boy inside that terrifying man, and how much he hated what he'd become. He'd followed all his compulsions and found nothing on the other side. He broke into a sprint, and I sprinted after him. I could run in a sky-high heel 17 *or* a Nike runner – never underestimate the power of a woman who can run in both!

I chased him and somehow backed him up against a brick wall. I could see the outline of my iPhone in his left jeans pocket. I wanted it back – I *needed* it back. There were thousands of videos and photographic evidence to prove Ed loved me when he was younger, and I needed those memories now he was a teen.

Now, readers, I do understand that at *this* point, or perhaps even earlier, most people would have cut their losses and let No Ears have the stupid iPhone. But I wasn't a cutter-of-losses sort of person and so I went him. Like a moth to a flame – like a goth at a ball game.

'Give me back my phone! I can see it. I've got a pair of secateurs in my pocket – I reckon that's what they cut your ears off with! *Secateurs!*'

Bingo!

He stopped moving, reached inside his pocket and dropped the phone. I caught it as it fell, and quickly started to film No Ears while he lunged toward me. Running backwards, I beat him to the car, got inside and locked the doors. He climbed onto the bonnet. The idiot, couldn't he see I was winning?

Once inside the Batmobile, my mood went full feral. I grabbed the car keys from my secret pocket, fired the ignition and floored it. He rolled right off like a stunt double, and I saw him stagger into a block of flats and disappear inside a stairwell.

I drove to the nearest police station, shaken and shattered, but somehow triumphant. The detective told me No Ears was a lost cause and that he was safer inside the system. The system? Is there a system? When someone like No Ears gets out of jail they go straight back to what they know: fumbled car burglaries. There was no freedom for people like No Ears. Addiction and trauma had wiped away all present and future love.

I drove home slowly, feeling sorry for No Ears.

The next day on my morning walk with Jack, we were both on the lookout. I wondered where No Ears had run to, and made sure my car was locked. The police had offered counselling, but why would I need counselling?

My lady secateurs had picked up a scent and we'd just found the best overhang I had *ever* seen. Magnolias, oranges, lavender and an abundance of red roses. *They'd really POP in my funeral parlour,* I thought. I stood on a nearby bright green milk crate and started to snip … eight red roses, snip snip, four lemons, snip snip … snip snip SNAP!

I heard a car screech to a halt beside me: a police car! Perhaps the police were helter-skeltering to let me know No Ears had been caught and was back inside the system.

'Hey! What are you doing? You're destroying public property. Where did you get that crate from? Get down off the crate!'

I didn't like the policeman's accusatory tone. *How* dare *you,* I thought … *How* dare *you tell* me *I'm a destroyer*!

My instinct was to sprint away like a red rose on ice … but then my special bird's-eye view came to the rescue.

Before I could answer a cocky yes to that inner voice, I heard a scream from the house next door. It was a posh-looking local, crying and shaking. She told the policeman she'd just been robbed. Out of nowhere a man had grabbed her handbag right off her arm in *broad daylight*!

Before the constable could open his mouth, I fired off questions. 'Was he alone, love? Did he steal money? What was he wearing? Have you seen him around here before? Are you all right, love? What was on his feet?' And finally, 'What did he look like?'

The woman cried, 'As weird as it sounds, he had *no ears*.'

Suddenly I was *all* ears!

The policeman was too. He seemed to have forgotten my snip-snip-snipping and turned his attention to someone who really needed it. And with that, I turned on the heel of my vintage Nikes and headed toward the beach, walking aimlessly. It's what loners do; we walk aimlessly.

Postscript: On the way home, I flirted with a dad pushing a stroller. I revisited one of the best overhangs I have *ever* seen and, you might be pleased to know, I went back and recovered the overhang, the one that was rightfully mine!

The brassiere of
lovelessness

Once, I bought a delicate French lace brassiere to make a man fall in love with me. I even bought undergarments to match so he'd *never* get over me.

The brassiere was silk-spun by a cult of designer spiders and blind merry widows. The brassiere promised a balcony that even Juliet could never fall from. The panties were high-waisted, with black gossamer threads lacing up on each thigh.

I had been a single mother for three years and, despite loving the delirium, independence and clarity that singledoom brings, before I could say 'Get me a bloody dummy', I was curious about dating all over again. I'm ashamed to say I was a little worried about Ed's baby crib (which looked exactly like a car seat, but with flowers) in the back seat of my car so I covered it with a blanket. I wasn't just a mother! I was back in the game and the baby crib was a dead giveaway.

I was like any other older single mother, in that my undergarments/smalls department required a massive overhaul. We single mothers let ourselves go in the undergarment/smalls department. We're what you might call 'all outside show'.

As a single, professional woman, I was *all* outside show. My exterior was flawless, although there was one small problem: it was time-consuming. It was taking me four times as long to look half as good as I used to, so by the time it came to my undergarments I thought, *Who cares, nobody is going to see my smalls.* Nobody would have *a clue* that underneath my dainty embellished frocks lay a horror show of beige bloomers, contour-shaping girdles, sexless Spanx, lace pettipants with cotton gussets, and three milk-stained maternity bras.

I'd taken to slipping into bed wearing flannelette nighties rather than silk nightgowns; I wore slippers, not high heels, and fluffy socks, not thigh-high lace stockings. In one year of single-motherdoom, I experimented further, wearing hair dye and a face mask to bed, gorging on packets of Smith's Crisps, a Picnic bar, mini Magnums and marshmallows while watching *Sex and the City* on repeat with no guilt! I'd stopped washing my sheets every week, and wore threadbare brassieres and panties to bed. I was a newly winged creature learning to fly. When ordinary life shackles me I escape toward another life, one way or another. But little niggly petticoat doubts were creeping in.

I believe it's quite natural for a single mother to start thinking about the difference between a dud and a hermit. A dud comes across as awkward, shy and a crashing bore. A hermit is highly intelligent, fumes without solitude and doesn't care if they offer anything to society. The hermit just wants to be left alone. The petticoat voices whispered, *Are you a dud or a hermit?*

Being single had some real high points, but it also led to some surreal and expansive behaviour. Like mad biddings at house auctions just to see if I'd win. I accidentally won a family-sized home in Armadale, and I didn't even *like* the family home but, unfortunately, by law I was obliged to buy it. To make up for my million-dollar mistake on a busy eight-lane highway, I hired a rather remarkable-looking tradie to knock down walls, rip out cupboards and replace the kitchen. Basically, to Alannahfy it.

I convinced myself that everlasting love and contentment were mine if I could get the hot tradie to fall in love with me. A tradie was the closest thing to Jesus, and *he* started off as a carpenter!

Tony Tones was fifteen years younger than me and was the proud owner of a spectacular well-structured jaw line. He had jet-black hair and piercing sea-green eyes and his teeth had no fillings. His model body glistened with man oil after hours in the sun and gym. His part-time modelling work required a fully sculpted body with what he called a 'rockin' Aussie tan'.

It was a full-time job hoodwinking him into loving me. On Valentine's Day, I delivered fifteen red roses with a love note to *myself*. The note said, 'Roses are red, violets are blue, I can't live another day without you!' Tony Tones and I had stepped out on four dates and I'd hoped the jealousy roses would turn his hand toward marriage! If Tony Tones showed any sign of jealousy, I'd won half the battle.

But *nothing*!

Instead, he carried the roses inside for me and lamented how he'd clean forgotten it was Valentine's Day.

One evening, after he'd expertly knocked down three walls, the garage and a bathroom/laundry, we had three pieces of lemon sponge cake topped with cream, and a cup of tea. He wanted a beer but I wanted tea and sympathy. He showed me childish drawings for a glittering new fishpond and a 'tranquillity garden'. Apparently, he knew all there was to know about property, and my million-dollar mistake would have *far* greater resale value with a Japanese garden. It was unsaleable without the Tony Tones touch.

Suddenly every light in the house went out for a moment, and in a total eclipse of the heart, in those few seconds of blackout, Tony Tones told me how he couldn't believe it, but he had feelings for me.

'You know something, girl, underneath all that clown make-up, you're a rockin' hot babe! Ever thought about a tan? You'd rock an Aussie tan!'

He continued as the lights flickered back on, 'Caaaaan't wait to build your garden ... I can do it for cash – around $40K should do it. Ya know you're going to end up on the cover of *Vogue Living*, don'tcha – black pebbles and small rocks, cacti – cement tiling – *relax*, I'll be on the cover with you, everyone's gonna wanna know who built the tranquillity garden.'

I didn't like tranquil Japanese-style gardens, and the idea of being on the cover of anything other than a fashion magazine was ludicrous. (Besides, I wanted a mad garden with lavender and overflow, lily ponds and moss and plum trees. And I wanted it to be fully grown in a month.) Yet I spontaneously decided his plan for my new garden would flow into eternal love.

Five months later the 'five-month stage' was coming up, and I'd failed to entice an 'I love you' or even an ironic 'You're gorgeous – let's get married' from his luscious tradie lips. If there's no 'I love you' by the five-month stage, your stress levels are sky high. You're erratic and start acting in really bizarre ways.

Tony Tones was not only a tradie – he was a plumber, landscape gardener, fountain designer, electrician, screenwriter, author, comedian, star footballer, star swimmer, star surfer, marriage counsellor (no certificates but he said he had clients), a male model in high demand and a Logie Award–winning actor. (He'd appeared in *Home and Away*, which to Tony meant he'd virtually won a Gold Logie.) He'd also appeared as himself in a film he wrote, directed, produced and edited called *Tradin' Up – Tradin' Down, I'm a Tradie not a Clown*. In my tradie-love state I believed it was the work of a genius – right up there with Ron Howard – and Tony Tones nodded in agreement. Tony Tones loved Ron Howard films. *American Graffiti* was his favourite.

We flew to Sydney and stayed at the Sheraton on the Park for the premiere of *Tradin' Up – Tradin' Down* at the Tropicana Short Film Festival, but at the last minute his premiere got bumped for a film about Aboriginal land rights.

Tony had been more than convinced he would be given the Young Directors Award but after he got bumped we walked back to the Sheraton empty-handed with no premiere and no award.

I'd never liked him more!

He made me a lemonade on ice after we arrived at our marriage suite, room 674. I felt sorry for him. This tradie was feelin' down!

Tradie up was nowhere in sight! He told me about his Oscars speech, the one he'd been practising in clients' mirrors for years.

An Oscars speech?

Tony disappeared and then reappeared from behind the door of the hotel bathroom. He'd changed outfits and was wearing a sparkling tuxedo jacket with tradie shorts. He dimmed the lights, asked if I was ready and then off he went ... for hours.

'Good evening, maaaates!'

(Pause to wipe a tear, with a disbelieving chuckle.)

'FUCK me, WORLD – I'm just a TRADIE from Broady ... a TRADIE FROM BROADY! I did ya proud, Dad – you TOLD me I wasn't just a tradie – I miss ya, Dad, ya old basdard, now LOOK at me, Dad, up here with an Oscar! Jesus, I can see Tom Cruise, if you or your religious mates ever need your lights rewired – I'm your guy. And TOM ... show me the MONEY!'

(He laughed a lot at that bit.)

(He then pointed to members of the pretend audience.) 'Bradley Cooper, Bradley Pitt, Colin Farrell and Leo di *Capriccio*. Maaaates! Just being in the same country as you guys gave me the hope, the DRIVE, to believe in meself.'

(He lit up a cigarette at this point. He needed time to prepare for his grand finale. He promised it would bring the house down.)

'Gary! Maaaaaaaate! You BELIEVED in my dreams ... you saw more than a tool belt. You knew I belonged in LA – fair dinkum, bro, I didn't win the Oscar, you did too! And to my BEAUTIFUL wife, my best friend, LOVE of my life, Amanda. Mandy! LOVE YA BABE! And our miracle IVF triplets – Bullet, Bruiser and Buster, love you guys! And remember this: the earth is big and the leaves are vast, the sea is green and the days pass … don't get old, don't get young – be like me, a FUCKING GUN!'

I was speechless. Had he forgotten he was rehearsing his future right in front of me? I comforted myself that he'd got the names confused. Alannah, Amanda – I could understand how, under pressure, it was easy to get the two confused.

But even after the Oscars speech, there was no 'I love you'.

I resorted to Bunnings. Tony Tones loved Bunnings and now I did too. I dressed down for Bunnings. Sequined frocks were not appreciated, and neither was my chandelier hairdo. I wrapped a velvet scrunchie around my hair, wore a pair of Blundstones on my feet, and wan, insipid lipstick on my lips. Tony Tones liked natural-looking girls, so I ditched my usual Ruby Woo red glossy lips after he assured me I could rock an un-glossed nude lip.

I circled Bunnings, offering advice to Tony Tones on how to grow cacti, how watering infrequently is important, and what's a weed and what's not a weed. I made all of my gardening information up as I went along, secretly scoffing four freshly cooked Bunnings sausages with onions and extra tomato sauce behind the fern section. Tony Tones was a vegetarian and so was I. But only if I was near him.

I wasn't expecting a Shakespearean play, or an award-winning sonnet. A Post-it note or two hand-picked daisies would have been enough. But after five months, if you haven't had an 'I love you' (said *with feeling*) and only a 'Love ya, babe, you're *soooo* good for me, it's bloody GREAT taking a break from dating models!' … it's time to run.

But I didn't. I couldn't let love beat me and so I limped on!

Listen up, dear readers, because I discovered that it all came down to my underwear. One dazzling evening, Tony Tones gave me a high five, pulled out a bong and asked me … 'Where's your gee-whizzer, girl? Gotta love a girl in a gee-whizzer.'

I asked what a gee-whizzer was. I planned to get one immediately.

Turns out a gee whizzer is a G-string. To put it mildly, I've never cared for a G-string. But I knew I needed to upscale my threadbare undergarments and my sexual magnetism, not just for Tony Tones, but for my loveable future.

Obviously the real problem was my out-of-date undergarments – those shaping corsets were holding back my tradie love. I knew I had to get to an Agent Provocateur lingerie store and fast.

I browsed the most beautiful lingerie I had ever felt my flesh goosebump for. In a hallowed enclave where cherubs re-string their bows, a vision hovered. This was the answer to all my prayers. An alluring silk-and-lace bullet brassiere promising lift, support and a smooth satin finish, with a gee-whizzer to match.

Gee whiz!

I hurried home to prepare. Tony Tones was due to appear in my boudoir at 8 pm. This would be the night when I finally captured all the love in his tradie heart.

I spent five hours preparing my single-motherdoom boudoir in the most romantic of stylings, plumping pillows and spraying lavender over the new 1000-thread-count sheet set. Surrounded by rose-infused candles and an antique lamp, I was suddenly fifteen years younger. I gently pulled on my black fishnet stockings, attaching them to the garter belt of love. The bullet brassiere was pure perfection – it was even called 'The Wonder Love Brassiere'. It had a satin bow at the front and was a spiderweb of black lace, lifting and separating like a miracle. The gee-whizzer, meanwhile, was causing all sorts of problems – it turns out I had it on back to front.

I lay on the bed, my Wonder Love bra perfecting the love-infused room. I was nervous but well prepared; I even had natural lip gloss hidden under the pillow. I heard the ticking of the downstairs clock and the first patter of rain. The clock ticked past 8 pm, past 9 pm – *he's a bit late*, I convinced myself … and then my phone beeped with a text.

Babe – you wood NOT believe this but I ran into Mandy today. Told you bout her???? Amanda? Anyways, she's back from LA. Her acting gig is not going grate, something big happened. Catching up with her for drinks. Catch ya later lol XX

I glared at the phone. I glared at the door. I glared at the floor. I glared at my bulletproof brassiere and then I glared at nothing. I was smarting with lovelessness. A bloody acting gig not going *grate* in LA. (Another failed *Home and Away* actor coming home, more like it!)

I'd been kidding myself. For five months, I'd turned my heart *inside* out and *upside* down all for nothing. I'd even been to Bunnings in a nude lip and listened to an Ocsars speech! I was a lyin' hypocritical vega-bloody-tarian.

THE BRASSIERE OF LOVELESSNESS

There is no love for sale in a Wonder Love bra, not even in a double D–sized cup. There's not enough support or underwire in the world to catch your fall. I thought if I didn't secure the tradie's love, I was worthless. But I was wrong.

I put Cat Stevens on the sound system and made a pretend martini (lemonade with a grape). I watched myself in the gilt mirror, all decked out provocateur-like in the muted bordello light.

And as fast as a screw can drill into a wall, I ripped off that gee-whizzer, deleted Tony Tones's number and screamed. I haven't seen his Oscar speech on television and there's a very good chance I never will!

ALANNAH HILL LAUNCHES 'LOVE ME TO DEATH' LINGERIE COLLECTION

Six months after the Brassiere of Lovelessness, I launched the 'Tease Me, Please Me, Love Me to Death' lingerie collection. The blush-pink lingerie featured bulletproof brassieres, cami-bloomers, and bias-cut 1940s silk slips. Models strutted down the catwalk holding giant balloons filled with helium love, jewelled *tool belts* on their swaying, rockin', love-me-to-death hips.

Not a gee-whizzer or a nude lip in sight!

I hadn't realised my own self-love was the real love I'd been craving. That was the real love I'd been missing. It was an expensive, humiliating lesson for me to learn.

Unrequited love can make a woman lose her instincts, power and judgement – it threatens to beat us down to a secret place where we hide curled up and wounded. But like a phoenix we rise from the ashes with more insight and wisdom than ever before.

After I got my power and instincts back I hired a professional tradie to complete the renovations on my million-dollar mistake. An elderly man from Jim's Gardening fixed up the 'tranquillity garden'. And the lingerie collection?

Gee whiz!

It was an Oscar-winning success!

Postscript: It's common practice for us women to let ourselves down in the underwear department, especially after a long relationship. My advice is to invest in your*selves*, my loves. You'll get far better returns.

The baby bonnet of *delusion*

I was doing what I always did: paddling underneath and forging ahead. Except this time I was paddling underneath and forging ahead with a little splash of baby vomit gracing my vintage lace.

Three weeks after my newborn dared to open his eyes and see the real world, I was a single mother creatively directing a super-galactic fashion house with electrifying new categories announced daily by the CEO.

These spine-tingling categories included Alannah Hill make-up, Alannah Hill manchester, Alannah Hill alcohol, Alannah Hill soaps, Alannah Hill swimwear, Alannah Hill tote bags, Alannah Hill tampons, Alannah Hill sunglasses … get the picture?

The CEO hid from me after the announcements, moving past me in shadowed, darkened hallways, looking everywhere but nowhere, and particularly *not* at me. He knew I was fuming at the rapid expansion of product lines. Fuming!

'KIDSWEAR!' he yelled. 'Alannah Hill kidswear! You've got a kid now, and guess what? Kids grow really quickly, so … ya know what I mean? KID$WEAR! Just shrink all the styles to kids' sizes. Get it? Course you don't, cos you don't listen. See that cardigan over there? Shrink it down, shrink everything down to zero and guess what? You got kidswear! Stop complaining, it's fuckin' easy. Got a great name for ya kidswear too – BUFFALO BILLS!'

I yelled back that I was far too busy for Buffalo Bills.

The staff ran in all directions, hoping to avoid the CEO's stream of sudden, manic changes issued to everything he'd already changed a week earlier. The phones kept ringing, couriers queued in reception, design assistants bitched, dogs barked and a group of Hells Angels appeared with a bong, demanding T-shirts be made. It was just another day of workplace mayhem – except I had my three-week-old baby fast asleep in a drawer.

I lied to myself about how well I was managing being a mother *and* a busy career woman. I lied to myself about how I was a staggering, phenomenal, blue-chip working mother, smashing it with everything I did for my brand-new son. Done up like a perfect Western Japanese doll 24/7, kitten heels on my feet, new baby attached to my hip, a painted smile hiding my thousand and one mistakes.

Delusion is very powerful and tastes incredibly sweet, much sweeter than the bitter aftertaste of reality. Delusion, for me, was the far better option, and for years I chose to live my life in a perfect imbalance with reality. Truth is, I was running on empty with a newborn baby asleep in a vintage armoire drawer and a career that defined my identity. I had no idea that my two loves might be incompatible.

I was convinced I was on top of everything! The brand needed me and I was very lucky that Edward could sleep in my office – I could tend to Ed and scramble for inspiration to design 1500 styles a year along with accessories, campaigns, press releases, new stores, fights and arguments *and* all the preparation for the Alannah Hill fashion shows.

I will admit, there were times I felt mighty sorry for myself. Crouched on a small couch, Edward wailing in my arms after another failed attempt to soothe him, a design assistant juggling one hundred glittery buttons between flickering fingers, wanting to know how many buttons went on the Cardigan of Sorrow – eight or ten? Ed wailing, patterns being made, incorrectly sized production flowing into the warehouse and twenty new Alannah Hill stores opening overnight.

I'd already decided nothing was going to stop me from holding onto my brilliant career. I thought I was lucky, having my baby at work. I didn't need a man. Ed needed a father, but I had my sister for support. And I'd hired a Mothercraft nanny.

I was a firm believer that women change after having a child – some for the better and some for the worse. I was also a firm believer that the chances of a first-time mother coming back into the workforce, especially in the highly strung, ever-changing world of fashion, and trying to be the same woman as before, well … those chances were slim. I would be the exception to the rule.

I lied to myself and almost believed it, as if the usual rules of career and motherhood didn't apply to me.

I needed people, and I was used to hectic hours. I'd been busy building a brand, and couldn't imagine staying home alone with a newborn. The soothing, the endless rocking, the feeding, the boredom, the thousand-yard stare into nothingness while pushing the baby silently through the local park. A woman's confidence is quickly shot into a cauldron of dirty nappies – and as for the baby talk? That wears very thin after two hours. And perhaps, for the very first time we begin to sympathise with our own mothers.

You'll note how, when you do, your own mother *glows* with the empathy she's been craving for years.

I was determined not to change, and to not go stark raving mad!

I was determined to be shining in the studio three weeks after having a baby. Re-entering the glittering world of fashion would not change a thing! No, not a thing. I would be on top of *everything*!

As well as the nanny, I immediately hired a housekeeper, a gardener, a pool cleaner and a therapist, and searched Google to chart a course through my everyday Google Earth chaos. And for a while, it looked like my juggling act was working. Until …

I naively took Edward on an overnight business trip to Sydney. He was two months old. I travelled alone without a pram or crib or a nanny, and I accidentally left him in the Myer manchester department in a lack-of-sleep trance while blithely trying on a new Dior *parfum*! Waking to a disappearing-baby nightmare, I found him right where I'd left him, smiling among the towels and sheets, such a good baby, dressed to kill in a knitted sherbet bonnet with bunny ears attached and a cherry-red velvet onesie – two small bows sewn on each snap button.

When Ed was six months old, I took on the single mother/career-woman role like a Mothercraft nurse on a broom. I had to fly to London and Paris on business, a round trip of fourteen days.

Easy!

I'd just hire an experienced nanny to travel with me and Ed.

Easy again!

The nanny came with five-star references, laughing, smiling and full of energy. She appeared to be very competent, baby loving and thoughtful. For the interview she brought a plastic container of homemade kiddie cookies. I was really impressed and gave her the job immediately. Unfortunately, she had exaggerated her skill set, and my instincts as a new career mother were a little off-key. As we were flying over Darwin she announced, 'I'm *so* bored … How much longer? I've never been past Sydney before and my head aches.'

Shortly after this, the nanny and Ed went missing. The kindly Qantas cabin manager shook me awake and whispered really, really quietly, 'Excuse me, Miss Hill. Very sorry to wake you, no need to panic, but your child and the young woman are missing … Try to relax.'

Relax???

I nearly stabbed him with a fork, but instead I ate two Valium and rolled onto the plane floor to immediately begin searching under the seats and all the overhead lockers, convinced Ed was trapped somewhere. I accused the staff and ten women of stealing him and, like a mother hen who had lost her chick, I pecked through that plane like no mother's business.

Edward was eventually found wrapped in a blanket near the galley, fast asleep. The nanny was eventually found in one of the secret flat beds in the stewards' sleeping area, an empty gin bottle in her hand, dressed in a Qantas uniform.

Upon arrival at Heathrow, we had agreed that the nanny would collect the bags – but after checking into our hotel our luggage refused to unlock. The code didn't seem to be working. That code would *never* work because they were not our bags. On close inspection the hostile bags in my room were clearly marked *Dr Judith Wales, Scotland*.

The nanny had picked up the wrong luggage, and Scotland was miles away!

Just like my damned breast milk – frozen in lost suitcases miles away!

I fell onto the hotel floor, cradling an insanely overwrought Edward in my arms. The Phenergan hadn't kicked in despite micro-dosing him and finally macro-dosing him over Singapore.

How was I going to work with a nanny who, the very next morning at the hotel buffet, informed me that she didn't like going out alone? She didn't think she'd like pushing a pram on the quaint streets of Knightsbridge, and Hyde Park was too big and creepy. She didn't feel safe on the London streets, not by day and definitely not at night. And certainly not with a newborn. She told me she didn't think she'd feel comfortable in Paris. Not even in the Luxembourg Gardens, where thousands of people had wandered safely for centuries.

She didn't feel safe anywhere!

My baby certainly wouldn't be safe with a nanny living with so much fear.

Unfortunately, she also didn't feel safe in the luxury hotel swimming pool or in any kind of toy shop, complaining that she missed her boyfriend and needed to phone him hourly. She needed to phone him hourly from my suite, with the charges billed to my room. It turns out the costs of telephoning your boyfriend hourly when you're in London and he's in Melbourne could fund an orphanage in Nepal for a year!

Why, she asked, were there were no playdates organised with French children and their posh English-speaking nannies in a castle or private home on the Rue de Rivoli? Why hadn't I organised playdates such as these instead of suggesting dangerous parks and dirty hotel swimming pools?

It was decided that the only place she felt safe was inside the hotel room and so that's where she'd stay, *all day*. Talking to her boyfriend. Hourly!

But when you're alone with your new bub in Paris on a business trip, and the nanny's gone rogue on the phone in your hotel suite, you have to get cracking. I got cracking and hired a French nanny to look after the Australian nanny I'd brought all the way from Melbourne.

Looking back on that remarkable and horribly expensive time, I wonder who I thought I was and what I thought I was achieving. Ed didn't need to travel halfway around the world in fourteen days, and he didn't need to have jetlag either. He would have been far more comfortable at home with my sister, who just adored him. So why did I put a nanny, Ed and myself through such an expensive trip, where so much of our time was spent literally up in the air?

I'll tell you why. I was showing off, desperate to prove I could forge ahead and do everything I used to do before I had a baby.

'Ohhhhhh … look at me with my tiny little baby … What's that, you ask? Yes, I'm a single mother. Oh thank you, yes, I *am* on fashion business with my newborn and a nanny. *Sorry?* Did you just ask if I'm Wonder Woman? No, but thank you for asking! And did you just say I'm *amazing?* No! YOU are! I'm a mother first but we've all got to earn a living somehow! Yes, yes … sure … the three of us have flown halfway around the world in fourteen days and *sure* it cost *a bomb.* It's really, *really* hard, but it's really, *really* worth it!'

It's *not* really, really worth it, dear reader, and don't let anybody tell you it is.

One of the secrets us mothers fail to grasp is that nobody cares if you *don't* take your newborn with you on a business trip halfway around the world. And nobody cares if you do either! But your little baby might rather *not* cavort through several time zones, flying over the whole of Russia.

In a wild attempt to prove I hadn't changed, I couldn't see a dummy for sense. We're not who we were before we had children and to even try to be is delusional! Nobody can do it all: the whole concept is a myth, and only makes women unhappy.

The trip to Europe was an unmitigated, rollicking, expensive, deluded, exhausting disaster. I nodded off with my mouth wide open in Topshop and got involved in some pram rage with five rude French nannies in the Luxembourg Gardens. We missed the flight home because the nanny didn't understand time zones. She thought 1300 was three o'clock, so Lanny, Nanny and Ed were stuck in the Heathrow Hilton Hotel for two days waiting for a flight home to Melbourne. I was in my design studio five hours after we landed, and Ed was jetlagged for weeks.

And the rogue nanny? She ran away!

Postscript:

Rock-a-bye baby on the treetop
When the wind blows the cradle will rock
When the bough breaks the cradle will fall
And down will come mother
Who can't do it all!

The handkerchief of *bravado*

You know the kind of nightmare where all your teeth – top and bottom – suddenly and unexpectedly disintegrate inside your little gob? Where your teeth implode like little towers of porcelain hit by a shot of acid, and the remaining mouthful of crunched-up cement forces you to become a statue of muted-ness?

These are the tooth-fairy queens of insecurity making their dawn raid on your sleeping psyche.

In your dream, Oprah had just asked you to write her next major speech on the meaning of life while Carl Jung, Charles Baudelaire and Enid Blyton congratulated you after your marvellously entertaining lecture on how dreams are a figment of the imagination and how Noddy *and* Big Ears really do exist (but only in your imagination).

The first part of the toothless dream is really, *really* lovely. Somebody is pressing their luscious, wet lips on yours – is it your old high-school crush? It doesn't matter, lips are brushing your starved, girlish pout, you're seducing a complete stranger and about to have the *best* kiss of your *entire* life, when … suddenly, a bomb goes off in your mouth, and it's not the sherbet kind.

Your hand slaps itself across your mouth, trying to stop your teeth falling at your new lover's feet. You try to kiss back but you can't – any slip of the tongue and your stumps will be revealed … you can actually feel your teeth splinter and then – thank God – in the nick of time, you magically wake up.

The relief is orgasmic.

Your teeth have *not* collapsed because of chronic insecurity. And they're not even a bit crumbly. Carl and Enid are not the *least* bit disappointed in you either. In the ghostly light of early morning, we comfort ourselves that our nightmare is only a dream.

But what if it wasn't?

We'd all be on life support or in a coma, more dead than alive.

Turns out that the toothless don't die from shame and shock. It turns out that even when facing social death, a thermos full of resilience kicks in. Despite our biggest fears, we somehow get through our worst nightmares with resilience and nerve.

How do I know, you ask?

Because I was once the crumbling, toothless leper.

After botched bridge work years earlier, a new Toorak dentist boldly announced that if I didn't do something quickly, I'd be toothless and bridgeless within a year.

I believed him, and agreed to his plan to build a bridge inside my mouth. Tiny titanium pegs were to be drilled into my gums and topped with porcelain crowns. In an English accent, the dentist said, 'Alannah, I *do* hope you're taking this seriously? This is a *three-month* procedure.'

'You're joking,' I said. 'Why *three* months? I have to go to Derby Day soon. Will my crowns be ready in time? I can't go to the races without a crown, love.'

'Patience, Alannah, patience. Your gums may be too weak to accept the pegs. The dental work will be done carefully, professionally and in four stages. First, we have to find out if your gums are weak.'

I nearly walked out. I didn't like hearing the word 'weak', especially in reference to me. The four stages sounded like wasted time when I could have been working. But I let him start the process even though I was anxious about my upcoming social calendar.

Derby Day has always filled me with anxiety. Years earlier, at the height of my success, if there was an A-grade do, I'd be thrilled to be invited but I'd rarely turn up. Being invited was enough. I stopped attending exclusive art openings and underground fashion shows. I *completely* forgot to RSVP to grand performances at the opera, and two front-row seats at the Australian Open were always empty. I'd rather watch the grand slam on television.

I secretly thought women over thirty-nine who attended two or more work-related events a week were over-ambitious.

I had to really push myself to attend social events, and the races were guaranteed nonstop boredom (especially when you don't drink). But I needed to show off my new brand, Louise Love, and Derby Day was perfect for hobnobbing.

I devised a four-hour social exit strategy to manage my time and escape route. Two hours for mingling, one hour spent in a bathroom and one hour's travel time. I spent weeks designing, redesigning and re-re-redesigning subtly outlandish one-off costumes for the Big Day. I'd spend hours turning silk spring-blossom fabric into Derby Day frights. The buttons and trims, all imported from France, cost a bomb, as did the flower bombs of silk to be spun onto my head. I hoped to be crowned Belle of the Derby.

I never wore any of my handmade costumes.

On the morning of the big day, I worried that my Belle of the Ball outfit wouldn't have the desired effect. That I was going to be the Chook of the Birdcage, not the Belle. I worried about looking like Esmeralda, the housekeeper from *Bewitched*, freshly escaped from the witch's home, raring to broom it to the Derby with all her ghostly friends.

And just like that, mid-eyelash curl, I lost my nerve.

Instead of wearing my hand-spun couture, I chose to wear an old favourite, an embellished frock. I used to think beaded frocks were the key to looking elegant at daytime social events. I liked to hide behind the thousands and thousands of shiny sequins, hoping the glare would mask my nagging anxiety and calm my disruptive urges.

As soon as my stilettos stepped onto the manicured lawn at Flemington, I realised my colossal mistake. It girls gazelled past wearing vintage Chanel, Dior and Balenciaga, intimidating me into wheeling out my B-grade personality … the one filled with phony confidence. Some of the gazelles were so overdressed, even I was impressed! Their fake tans were flawless, while my foundation number two full-body cover was beginning to form small cracks, unmasking a violet-coloured vein spreading like fire on my right leg. My lace sockettes, I observed in the harsh light of day, were beginning to fray, and my dress appeared to have dog hair attached to each blingy sequin. Worst of all, I swear I felt two or three of my temporary crowns move slightly every time I said a word beginning with 'S'. A lot of my B-grade personality was made up of S words so I was careful not to spit when I hissed superb, scream, suck up, shivers, sexual, shallow, sheep or sympathy.

As glamorous as I may have appeared to be, I wasn't a mani-pedi type of girl either. I didn't think anybody would notice my unmanicured hands flailing about in the Birdcage, and I wouldn't be seen alive or dead wearing a boring open-toe sandal, so why waste time with the mani or the pedi? *Big* mistake! The manis and pedis are highly regarded in the Cage – you're even judged on them. Shiny, plastic hands gleamed all around me, world-class mani-pedis shining in the summer heat while my freckled hands sported wafer-thin splintered fingernails and eye-shadow remnants just behind one nail.

But as it turned out, nobody noticed my lacklustre hands.

My photo was taken with Miranda Kerr for the social pages, and it confirmed my worst suspicions. A 54-year-old fashion designer, arriving alone in a chauffeured car to the extravagant Derby Day in a bobby sock, with foundation-covered legs and wearing an 'old favourite', was attired completely inappropriately.

I felt like mutton dressed up as Lan.

In preparation for the big day, I'd spent a fair whack of time perfecting red-carpet poses. Unfortunately, I modelled my poses on Kim Kardashian (160 million Insta followers can't be wrong). I'd read how Kim attended a celebrity boot camp for A-grade posing called 'Posing Is a Performing Art'. Kim shared how she studied the art of thrusting out one collarbone and pulling half her body back while *at the same time* draping her overrated, rather short legs around a garden gnome, sucking in her cheeks, pursing her lips, flicking her head and hair, pulling her stomach in and arching her back *while* pushing her bottom out at a 90-degree angle.

You can imagine what I looked like in the *Herald Sun* social pages the next day. I barely recognised myself.

Mutton dressed up as Lan, posing as Kim.

But it got worse.

With my B-grade personality, I'd been trying to impress the newly hired gun CEO at David Jones. I knew just seconds into our conversation that with my fine reputation and winning smile (the temporary teeth hidden), my social awkwardness tricked up with bravado would be seen as unique business savvy. Intuitively, I was a little off balance and skittish. I was witty and fashion-inquisitive, with a lively interest in the recently plummeting share price of DJs stock. I was veering the CEO onto a rose-petalled path, turning questions into answers, back into statements, and then into a sudden 180-degree turn that had nothing to do with anything while also making stunning observations about his marriage.

He was intrigued, and waved two other fashionistas away. Louise Love was on his mind.

The CEO and I were sipping warm sparkling wine when my first crown flew the coop. Mid-sip, the crown just popped out of my mouth and into my sparkling wine. I heard it go plop and, panic-stricken, I thought about fainting. Was I dreaming? No, I was wide awake!

The CEO didn't see the first tooth fall. With my quick Tassie reflexes, I scooped the tooth out of the wine with my tongue, expertly flicking it back into its stump.

I heard nothing but the rush of social shame.

The CEO rattled on, smiling. I smiled, he smiled. I hoped the tooth would stay put. Unfortunately, my mind was locked onto words beginning with S. I told him how Superb my new brand was, and how he'd Scream and Shiver at the chic Styling that was *sooooo* Sophisticated.

Just after I said 'Sophisticated', two of my temporaries hurtled themselves toward his open mouth. I tried to fall into the ground, through the ground and, hopefully, completely disappear. I heard his voice:

'Hey, Alannah … I must be drunk. I'm so sorry, for a second there I thought I saw flying teeth!'

I didn't say a word.

With one *unmanicured* hand over my mouth, I took the risk of a half-smile, hoping against hope that the pegs would not reveal themselves.

The DJs CEO recoiled. I and my fascinator recoiled with him.

I had three to four seconds to redeem myself. I fell to the Birdcage floor, grabbed my two flyaway teeth and snatched two white peppermint Mentos out of my overflowing handbag. I chewed the two Mentos frantically (Mentos, it turns out, are very hard to chew when delirious with stress) and after cleverly tonguing the two half-eaten mints over the stumps in my mouth, I rose from the floor of that Cage like a wretched contumacious seagull who'd just found God.

I mumbled a farewell and headed straight for the exit, flying out of the Birdcage on my Esmeralda broom, a linen hanky over my mouth, straight into the safety of my waiting car, where I pretended to fall asleep on the black leather seat.

Would I ever recover?

I'd lived through one of my biggest fears and yet here I was, still alive, in the back seat of a chauffeured car. Outside, everything seemed normal. All the traffic lights were still turning red and green and back again. By the time I got home, I'd realised we are stronger and more resilient than we give ourselves credit for.

I often wonder how people manage to soldier on when really terrible things happen. *Truly* terrible, life-changing things, like mothers who lose a cherished child. I honestly do not know how those mothers take another breath, but they do. Husbands lose wives, wives lose husbands, children leave parents behind, girlfriends lose boyfriends, partners disappear, our teeth fall out and we think we will never recover.

But we do recover, we do survive.

I'd only lost a couple of teeth, after all, and with a little bit of *patience* they could be fixed.

We have a choice: our world is split between taking risks and staying small. I'm not convinced real spiritual growth happens on a yoga mat or climbing the Himalayas with a goat in a flower-spangled coat! Real spiritual growth happens when we least expect it. When we're forced to navigate the road ahead even if our most feared nightmares dare us not to.

Postscript: I don't have the crumbling teeth nightmare any longer. I have a brand-new one!

I am a hair fairy with my hair falling out in clumps. A girl tries to stick the clumps onto her own head. She's blonde. I see scissors. I duck. Too late, the girl snips. She snips again. Her name's Delilah! I'm bald in the dream now, and my baldness reveals hundreds of large freckles and moles. Delilah tells me she's a dark star and a head manipulator, and is only trying to change my destiny.

I cough. A furball falls from my gob … and then I wake up. Thank God I'm not blonde or bald! And I have to remember Delilah isn't the enemy hindering my progress in life. She's just the fairy godmother of insecurity, making another dawn raid on my sleeping psyche.

The gumboots of *mayhem*

Make no mistake about it: from the moment you walk through the primary school gates with your tiny tot fearfully clutching your shaking hand, you're being judged, and your character, clothing, hairdo and make-up are ripped apart like a manic monkey shreds a hairy coconut.

It takes less than five minutes to be judged. And once you're typecast at primary school, it's very rare to be recast – the type you're given follows you all the way through to Grade 6 and, if you're really unlucky, to the dizzy heights of Grade 12! It's not fair but that's the state of affairs, I'm afraid!

The first thing you discover is that there is one group who are clearly Friends Of The School. In my quest to do the best by my son, I aspired to be part of this group – in fact, I busted my heart to be a Friend Of The School, but it didn't go as well as I hoped because there are FOTS, and then there are people like me.

FOTS make parenting look effortless, pushing the right pram in a sensible runner or Birkenstock. I was more of an unnatural mother – chaotic, impractical, capricious and unFOTSy. Unnatural mothers *wither* in full daylight, pushing the wrong pram in Prada heels. Unnatural mothers serve up mini Magnums for breakfast and make parenthood look like a nuclear explosion. Basically, FOTS belong to a traditional, rational, nuclear family *fixated* on climate change and saving the planet. They have political correctness down pat and healthy lunches that don't make their kiddies fat!*

Working out what type of school parent you are is a very serious matter – you can't pretend you're one of the FOTS when you're *not*. As a new school mum, I psychoanalysed the parents and worked out the types pretty quickly:

SAM: Single Arty Mother (I was immediately cast as a SAM)

SAD: Single Arty Dad

WAD: Warring And Divorcing

RAD: Rock's Absent Dad

SHD: Stay-Home Dad

RADs were scarce at Ed's primary school. I liked to think a RAD's cavalier attitude toward parenting (replacing children with guitars) would suit my parenting sensibilities. However, I don't appreciate guitars or a rock-god vibe … and if a RAD turned up wearing a leather pant, *forget* it.

A WAD told me RADs are *always* late for school assembly, often arriving without their child's schoolbag, *without* their child's lunch and once, without their *actual* child! When Tex Perkins was a RAD at the school, he once played a tune for the annual Jazz in the Park and flirted wildly with a group of SAMs. It's a real shame I missed out on schoolyard advice and lingering flirts with a RAD – a RAD and I could have been imperfect, flirtin' parents together.

---

* The school's philosophy on food had me panicked me from day zero. Sugary snacks were abolished, fairy bread denounced, fruit with pips outlawed, and peanut butter blacklisted (I quickly discovered peanut butter does hold traces of real nuts). *Any* sign, any trace, any sniff, any whiff of *any* kind of a nut in your child's lunch box and you're seen as 'reckless' and 'negligent' and entire families avoid you and your nutty mistake for years.

The school might not have had many RADs but we did have a Trev: Trevor Marmalade, the comedian from *The Footy Show*. I really liked Trevor Marmalade. I made marmalade jam jokes around him, but it was our snide wicked smirks and stuffed-in laughter at the school assembly where Trevor and I really jammed! His two children were gorgeous, and his wife always had a moment for me. Trev changed groups four times in six years – unheard of! He started off as a FOTS, turned into a WAD, morphed into a RAD and, last I heard, Trev's now a SAD.

FOTS can be found in school playgrounds, working covertly in cahoots with the principal, the vice principal and the gardener. The school sees FOTS as so responsible, they're permitted to manage school working bees, hold fundraising competitions and teach after-school programs like 'Still Breastfeeding Your Twelve-Year-Old? Well Done, Mum!'

In other words, FOTS rule the school.

With their strong opinions, wild woolly hair and careful charitable hands, FOTS can appear Jesus-like – except unlike the real Jesus, FOTS turn up for Christmas, Easter Sunday *and* Good Friday. FOTS are shining beacons of hope channelling PC messages from God, and they're not nailed to a cross, they're wearing organic T-shirts emblazoned with WHAT DID YOU DO TO SAVE THE PLANET TODAY?

I felt this was a direct message to people like me. Me and my hairspray were obviously directly responsible for ruining the planet. I didn't have political correctness down pat and was still becoming accustomed to the concept of recycling. I used the green bin for everything.

At my son's school, it was not uncommon for me to see a full-blown FOTS mum with three ginger-haired kiddies squashed inside a homemade wooden go-kart attached to a bicycle barrelling toward me. The entire FOTS family would be sporting rip-roaring heat rashes, munching on organic carrots and wearing sun hats bigger than the sun; it was enough to give me a spider-bite rash without the spider.

FOTS make their own cream for their rip-roaring heat rashes and are not only expert in organising working bees, school fetes and school sports days, they volunteer for *everything*. FOTS can raise an eyebrow so high it almost disappears if they spot your dog off its leash and, wouldn't you know it, they even scoop up the dog poo, even when there's nobody around. (I once spied a FOTS throwing dog poo into a yellow recycling bin. I raised one of my own eyebrows, because even I knew the yellow bin wasn't for dog poo.)

Time becomes a clock with runaway hands when you're a single, career-driven mum. But I was aching to be seen as a number-one FOTS mum, so any chance I could get away from the design studio, I shadowed the school. When it was my turn to be a 'parent reader' I showed up with bells on, and when I turned up for show-and-tell I distracted Ed's class with my Halloween face and witch's mask. (Ed's class apparently thought I was a witch, so I went along with the vibe for six more years.)

I found the time once to drive behind the school bus to surprise Ed and his friends when they arrived at school camp. A FOTS mum texted me three kilometres in and told me to turn back. I obeyed, immediately. I was known for breaking boundaries but FOTS were known for setting them. A FOTS's power has no boundaries! The car-parking rules for the 3.30 pm school pick-up were non-negotiable and to get a primo spot it was well advised to arrive an hour early. Double parking or parking in the principal's spot earned an immediate handwritten note. The note reminded you to be respectful, and that *you know* how important setting a good example for your child is. I'd do my level best *not* to double park in front of a fire hydrant or block in a BMW in my race to pick up Ed on time, but sometimes, you know how it is … I couldn't wait to see Ed's face through the classroom window and so I received quite a few of the 'rules and respect' notes.

I also knew how to get all the kiddies' attention. As soon as they saw my witchy face swanking toward their classroom they'd be standing on their desks, pointing and chanting, 'It's Ed's mum! Do the *Alannah Dance* … do the *Alannah Dance* … do the *Alannah Dance!*'

The Alannah Dance was created when I was a slip of a girl: a show-off move I used when I was bored and wanted to shock, or when I was feeling shy and wanted to divert attention away from my real self. It was a big hit in my early twenties, but in my forties the Alannah Dance was very likely a mistake. I did the dance to let Ed and his entire class know that not only was it almost home time but that Mother *of the Year* had arrived to snatch a few children away for a playdate!

Not many of the FOTS were aware I had the uncanny ability to walk and pelvic thrust at the same time. With eighty mum eyes boring into my show-off back, I danced like a female Elvis, pelvis thrusting and gyrating across the quadrangle until the kids' chants were a mini roar. Stepping forward, I'd thrust my pelvis out with exaggerated force, and on the backward step, thrust my pelvis back. I was better than a go-go dancer with ants in her pants. Both arms worked with each pelvis thrust and I liked to wave mine around like I didn't have any. On special days I'd let fake blood dribble from my mouth and, God, how the kids screamed as I lay dying outside their classroom after thrusting myself into a near-death experience.

'I'm bleeding to death … I need BLEEDING help! Call the paramedics, kids!'

The mums' eighty eyes were the size of eighty full moons.

I know what you're thinking, and I know it sounds theatrical and a little mad. But when you've had a childhood where love was never seen, you can either shrink yourself to nothing or exaggerate in expansive ways like a three-tier sponge cake with rich cream, lemon icing and a cherry on top. The school playground is a psychiatrist's maze of emotions, with mums and dads playing out old patterns and watching history repeating itself in real time.

I tried to change my history.

I'd throw myself into schoolyard conversations with some of the FOTS mums. It was the perfect chance to show them I was really one of them! All they had to do was look behind my chandelier hairdo – just as you can't judge a book by its cover, you can't judge a mother by a chandelier hairdo. You never know what's teased up inside! But, being uncertain, I'd wait before throwing my hairdo and fluttering words into any conversation the FOTS might be having. And then: 'Do you *ever* have that *awful* nightmare … the *awful* nightmare where your child disappears?'

In the eerie silence that followed, I offered gifts from my bag – banana peel and chocolate and inedible hummus dip. If my personality and hairdo couldn't win them over, my offerings would.

'Oh, Shereeeee! Death nightmares have *tortured* me for years,' I carried on. 'I see policemen walking with weighted urgency toward my custom-made pink door – by the way, love, you should *see* my front door … it's sherbet-bomb pink. Pop over some time. I could cook homemade takeaway and then show you the door.'

'What colour is sherbet bomb?' a mum asked. 'It's not in the Derwent coloured pencils.'

I couldn't help noticing the FOTS mums were not dipping banana peel into the hummus dip or gobbling any chocolate. One asked whether I preferred to grill or barbecue, and did I make my own pastry for Christmas quince pies? I knew to change the subject when she brought up sautéing, Jamie Oliver and baking. Baking was key to being a FOTS and a baker I was not!

Not one mum took up the offer of viewing my custom-made front door and homemade takeaway. As a single working mum, did I want to come home after working all day to make chicken 'cock-oh-van'? Lobster purees? Bangers 'n' mash? Tortellini al ragu? Or a sautéed quince pie?

No! Of course, I didn't! Not many mothers do! Do they?

I baked-beaned on and hoped I was fitting in. 'Oh loves, what's the world without imagination, love and realism … you've *honestly* never dreamed the love of your life, your adored child, is suddenly and unexpectedly taken from you? Never dreamed that? *Ever?*'

The question sucked all the oxygen off the sports oval. The FOTS quickly splintered off on bicycles, a labradoodle puppy running obediently behind one. Clearly FOTS had a problem with my uplifting, witty conversation and were running from the very thing they feared most … a deathly fear of death.

A FOTS husband is heavily involved in the school. They're often called Dave or Colin and are hardworking, FOTS-pecked and agreeable. A Dave or Colin usually works from home and yet no FBI mum has ever been able to find out what they actually do. I'd given it my best shot but even stickybeak me couldn't get to the bottom of it. My feeling was a FOTS husband hid out in a man shed in the backyard where he tinkered with broken computers, checked the weather, drank craft beer and watched the cricket on an old TV.

One FOTS father, after my ten-minute interrogation in the school sandpit, confessed he'd found a kilo of pot sewn into the lining of his favourite leather jacket, a leftover from his bachelor years. He'd been writing a future bestseller in the family attic about how goblins, ants and ragdoll kittens will eventually save the planet. In between his household chores, washing and ironing, vegie gardening, cooking, school pick-ups and coaching school basketball, he said he didn't get much time to himself or the 'serious pot smoking' his novel required. He estimated he'd have a first draft completed by the end of 2044.

A Dave or Colin, without any notice or council permits, could arrive in a tip truck with a cement mixer, and in one afternoon … they've made a pizza oven, poured concrete for a new basketball court and built two temporary classrooms. They micromanage the school's vegie garden – lettuce, carrots, silverbeet, potatoes and tomatoes – and see 'real commitment' when they observe a working SAM donating her precious spare time to help out. I loved the idea of the school vegie garden. I could see Ed playing while I gardened so I asked ten times if I could help.

My gardening outfit was impressive: pink Miu Miu gumboots, cherry-red stockings, a black bow-embellished skirt, a silk floral camisole with a sequinned navy-blue cardigan. A head scarf tied in a huge bow topped my garden head. I wore overalls over my costume. I wanted to be taken seriously. Unfortunately, it was unFOTS-friendly.

I could see that Dave-or-Colin was doubting my potential, which was when the little pink lies slipped out, one after the other like tiny garden gnomes. Of *course*, I knew a weed from a plant. Of *course*, I was an expert in all aspects of vegie gardens. I was also an expert pruner of lemon trees and rose bushes, I told him, as further proof of my green thumb. The agreeable FOTS dad told me to get straight into that vegie patch and get *straight* into weeding it, so I did! I weeded out all the weeds – everything looked like a weed to me. If it was green, it was a weed!

I was downcast when Dave roared at me, a kiddie on each hip and a newborn trapped in a Baby Bjorn on his front. It turns out that young carrots and tomato plants look exactly like *green weeds*!

I didn't like that vegie patch anyway.

By the time Ed was in Grade 3, I was more determined than ever to create a new type of group. It would be called HOME: Hopeful Overdone Mum Eccentric.

I felt the mums who drank wine at 9 and not at 5 needed a new group, with *me* as their leader! I would be the *responsible* teetotalling one. The good one. Sadly, I never got the numbers for the HOME group despite years of trying.

Spending time with Ed's 'fun mum' (me) was a real treat for some of the kids and, in one family, it was a reward for being good: 'If you're good you can go to Alannah's house but only *for half an hour!*'

But with my overdone personality I had to be very careful not to overdo it. It meant simultaneously entertaining Ed and a few kiddie friends while answering emails from suppliers and fuming over daily disasters at work while being aware that any 'untoward antics' might be reported back.

I encouraged the kids to play with make-up and gave deportment and grooming lessons, organised Gold Class cinema visits, treasure hunts, birthday parties in hot-pink Hummers, $8-a-cup lemonade stalls on Fitzroy St (I was teaching Ed and his friends the value of money), busking on Chapel Street at midnight, writing poetry, talking about feelings and playing dress-ups.

But my big hit (other than the Alannah Dance) was a game I invented called Murder. It was played in the infamous Fawkner Park (conveniently opposite my haunted mansion on Toorak Road). Fawkner Park is known for being haunted – a park where lost spirits and ghosts roam long after midnight. I always played the lead in Murder, and like all leads in these sorts of games we search for kids hiding behind bushes, carrying a huge black knife with fake blood dripping off its shiny blade. The part of the game I loved the most was sending Ed and his playdates a spooky selfie on their phones to make them shake with fear while they hid. My face was done up to look like a witch, and I would send the kids the gruesome selfie followed by a text message:

MURDER KNOWS WHERE YOU HIDE

And off I'd go into Fawkner Park with a torch to fake murder with my fake bleeding knife.

But

because the park was so big, one midnight moonlit evening, a kiddie got lost for an hour.

Parents were telephoned. Text messages were sent. One parent called an ambulance. (*Un*called for, I thought.)

I was exposed as an 'irresponsible scaremongering mother' and the Murder game was shut down. I tried explaining how harmless the game was and how fear could build *real* courage in children if they were open to it. The other parents completely disagreed. All of them! Such a shame. The kids loved it.

Upon reflection, waving a fake bloodstained knife and chasing kids around a city park at night was perhaps not the best move for an aspiring FOTS.

Instead I donated money to the school library along with a tonne of brand-new Alannah Hill clothing for the dress-up box. I'd even designed a marble plaque to adorn the new besser-block eyesore of a library and waited for the hand-delivered letter from the school principal to inform me when the plaque would be going up.

With everlasting thanks
to ALANNAH HILL

Philanthropist & Benefactor of Books
PATRON SAINT of Berserk Mothers

That letter was just around the corner. I could almost smell the gratitude! It smelt like freshly cut roses …

Postscript: Make no mistake about it, school parents: if you feel like a misfit you probably are. If you feel overdressed, you probably are. If you feel underdressed, you probably are. And if you feel nervous, you should be! The school ground is crowded with tall people making you feel small – tall mums with more judgement than a church full of nosy nuns at a cocktail party. My advice is to start campaigning for a Hopeful Overdone Mum Eccentrics group at your school immediately. Gather the other misfits close to your misfit soul. If you start in prep there's a very good chance you might get the numbers. Start campaigning now, my loves, and make that HOME group yours!

The killer heel of
utopia

Shoes!

Tell me about your shoes and I'll tell you who you are.

Tell me about *my* shoes and I'll tell you who I'm not.

You can tell a lot about a person by their shoes, *especially* if you're a natural-born stickybeak and *incredibly* judgemental. Needless to say, I have perfected the art of judging people by their shoes.

In my hometown of Geeveston, Tasmania, everyone wore the same shoes day after day, year after year, whether it was Christmas, Good Friday or Sunday bloody Sunday. The two exceptions were Mrs Anderson, who stood tall and glamorous in her shiny high heels for special occasions, and Mrs Dickens, who occasionally stood short and angry in her husband's green gumboots.

I've *always* judged people on their shoes, so it's no wonder that I own sixty pairs of unwearable, expensive bejewelled shoes. My shoes are treated like the crown jewels, opulent and unattainable. They're displayed on pink glass shelves inside a locked showcase in a Florentine dresser in my Florentine bedroom.

On the top shelf, a pair of black sparkling Miu Miu kitten heels with a blush-pink fur ankle strap sit next to a pointy-toed crème vintage-lace pump set on a 95 mm leather-covered stiletto. And right next to them are a divine pair of Jimmy Choo bejewelled pink satin-ribbon sky-highs, and a pair of Dolce & Gabbana sparkling silver platforms, with a cut out in the actual platform making them more of an art piece. The lower shelf features bejewelled Prada platforms, gilded gold-leaf Gucci stilettos and a pair of super elegant Valentino bridal sky-highs. With bows!

I bring them out sometimes to remind myself how shoe-mental I am.

And like all shoe-mental woman, I only wear three pairs of my shoes and a slipper. Slippers are not shoes and hopefully will never be classed as such! I wear a pair of floral Dolce & Gabbana bejewelled platforms, a well-worn runner (sneaker), black patent-leather Prada ankle boots and a pair of blush-pink slippers with a bunny's face that I bought for $10 in Chinatown! Most women don't wear half the shoes they own, and nobody really understands why. Like a kite chases the wind, a shoe addict chases the rush of buying their first pair. I think it's why so many of us have so many pairs ... we're heel-to-toe addicts, we have to keep going back for more!

There isn't a scientist or psychiatrist who can grasp the mind of a functioning shoe-oholic. Carrie from *Sex and the City* believed that a new pair of shoes fixed her blues and unpaid rent, stomping along Fifth Avenue in a pair of Jimmy Choos or Manolo Blahniks. I, too, used to fool myself a new shoe could fix my blues, but after my forty-seventh pair I knew a shoe could only fix a high-heeled burning heart for an hour or two.

A high heel can be a woman's Achilles heel. Mastering a high heel is as much about mental comfort as it is physical. If you *think* you can't walk in high heels, you probably can't … you've given up too easily, and already lost the battle.

I couldn't be seen *without* a high heel dangling from my legs, and after decades of wearing the sky-highs, I was numb to the blistering discomfort, back pain, neck cranking, foot swelling, loss of balance, dizziness and extreme short temper associated with the searing pain a sky-high brings.

No fashion adornment has kicked its way into our psyche like the shoe. Take Cinderella, for example. Without her glass slipper, she would have been a *complete nobody*, and Dorothy would have been left to die in Kansas without her ruby slippers.

You may well be asking yourself, 'I wonder what *my* shoes say about me?'

Perhaps your shoes are scuffed and well worn; maybe you're wearing an apologetic brown sandal, a vintage Nike runner, or a handmade English brogue. Maybe you've chosen the underrated mule, or a knee-high leather boot, or a kitten heel.

Let me share what I've learnt from decades of being judgemental about shoes and their wearers.

Hush Puppies and Dr Scholls are worn by people who can't form real relationships – they're often emotionally depleted, aloof and repressed. The Hush Puppy wearer cares what others think of them and dresses to please but, generally speaking, they just want to blend in and live a safe, average, normal life.

A lace-up brown brogue belongs to a slow-walking oncologist bearing nothing but bad news.

A pricey Prada or Gucci loafer is worn by someone with a high income and maxed-out credit card, vain gloriousness and selfish unreliability rotting their very core.

The sexy minx favours the knee-high leather boot or kitten heel.

A ne'er-do-well gives themself away with showy coloured shoes, while a bejewelled sparkly shoe belongs to a social extrovert.

A *really* well cared-for shoe signifies a social *introvert*.

A plain loafer belongs to a conscientious, socially inept person, usually divorced or about to commit adultery.

The wearer of a *good* runner is a freedom-seeker and open to all sorts of far-flung possibilities.

For those who've *completely* given up, an ugg boot or cheap thong (or flip-flop) from Kmart is generally favoured, while sock-wearing thongers are usually men suffering from low self-esteem, wary of heavy lifting and clueless about how to manage money. (To be honest, I don't rate the thong as an actual shoe, but I appreciate it when a thong wearer pairs socks with their thong – a look still struggling to catch on!)

I call the ugg the 'ugh' or 'ugly' boot – two little dead, eviscerated sheep impaled on your feet, and it's flat-soled to boot! A flat mixed with an ugg, *ugh*!

Mirror, mirror, on the wall, who's the ugliest of them all?

The *ugg*!

(Rumour has it a new law has just been passed. If an ugg-boot wearer is caught wearing uggs in public, it's immediately five years' jail – at least in my book!)

I told you I was shoe-judge mad!

Hopefully, you're the kind of woman who wears a 14-centimetre killer high heel, because I was the kind of woman who wore 14-centimetre killer high heels.

When I discovered the power of the high, high heel, the gods transformed me into something other than human. I was elevated, up high, *confident* as Lady Muck on stilts. I could text, hum a ditty and drink a can of Diet Coke in a pair of killer heels.

I admire the power of high heels. Once our feet are trapped inside, we're forced to walk with confidence and determination, the high heel elongating our legs and the curve of our calf muscles. Heeled up, we walk bolt upright, our chests thrust forward. The power of the heel is so exalting, it elevates us upon a pedestal, taller and nearer to God. Heels command attention and bestow presence on every social occasion. A flat shoe gives absolutely no presence to any social occasion – they're too boring and too *flat*. People who wear flats are discontented back-stabbers, whereas the high heelers are born warriors. A well-dressed woman in a high heel can wield power over any man in any position in life!

People think high heels are cruel for the feet, but the ballet flat is the real cruel shoe. A ballet flat's entire existence is based on a lie, making you believe you will now be as graceful and refined as a ballerina. The ballet flat takes *full* advantage of our childhood dreams. You're *not* a ballerina just because you wear ballerina flats, you're just a shorter, dumpier version of yourself … and you'll *never* be a Black Swan!

Cruel, girls!

I've *never* seen a fashion model exude confidence, strength and a look-at-me-while-I-storm-this-catwalk vibe in a pair of boring old flats, have you? You simply cannot stampede anywhere with confidence in a ballet flat – you need the high heel, and a fear of falling, to propel you forward. I wore a pair of ballet flats for ten minutes a few years back and I've never felt more passionless, useless and closer to the devil in all my life.

And then there's the *clog*! Clog are worn by kind, delusional women, often in a state of climate-change panic from which there can be no escape. They ride their fixed-gear bicycles in circles, looking for the next rally. A committed clog wearer doesn't believe in body-hair removal, they don't flush toilets, they don't care for a sugary milkshake or a Boston bun, and the tofu *must* be organic along with every other aspect of their existence. A clog wearer has morals and strong opinions, and they don't wear clothes made in China. I'm yet to see a man wearing the clog. If I ever do I might have to report him to the police.

Did you know the clog was *originally* designed as protective footwear for people working in factories in Sweden? People think the clog is a sign of freedom, but in reality it's a symbol of *poverty*.

I wouldn't be caught dead in a clog!

For me, it was *all* about the high heel.

The Alannah Hill brand without a killer high heel would have been just another whimsical women's clothing brand. Shoes are *crucial* in completing any outfit, and being shoe-mad and full of ideas, I asked my business partner, Factory X, to invest big money in an Alannah Hill killer high-heel collection.

My design assistant, Amy, found a shoe factory in Spain that made shoes for Dolce & Gabbana. I knew about heel heights, crystal baubles and ornamental shoes, but I had no idea how to design a 14-centimetre stiletto heel. Being an excellent mentor and problem-solver, I knew exactly what to do! Amy would complete an online crash course in 'how to design killer high heels'. A killer idea that worked! The killers sold out, and the following season the shoe budget was upped by one million dollars.

Ten new killer sky-high styles! I was *killing* it!

I'd shoo this in, I'd kick up my heels and do a tip-tap-toe in my sky-highs. I knew all about shoes and what women wanted.

So, how did I get it so wrong?

From the height of CEO heaven, *ballerina flats* were rudely and outrageously dropped into my high-heeled world. It was all Miu Miu's fault. I was savvy enough to know that if Miu Miu's new collections featured the dreaded flats, *everybody's* new collections would feature flats. It's one of the reasons I didn't care for the revolving world of fashion. One minute people wanted to be up high, and the next they were happy to be flat on the ground!

I naively agreed to a 'shoe focus group think tank' arranged by a store manager who knew heel-to-toe nothing about shoes. My focus-group thinkers were three store assistants, an eighteen-year-old intern from a PR company and the wife of the warehouse manager, who apparently knew *everything* there was to know about shoes. *I* knew everything there was to know about shoes, not *them*! But I was at *least* prepared to listen to their low-heeled feedback. (I was good like that!)

The focus group's feedback was presented on a flat piece of paper. The data they'd collected (from Lord knows where) suggested that ten pairs of killer heels could alienate and divide customers. Apparently, I needed to diversify, and embrace exciting new ideas like ballet flats. The think-tankers said not *everybody* wanted to look like me; in fact, some people wanted to look the opposite.

I nearly flattened the lot of them!

Everyone knew not to mention the word *flat* around me! I could have a *highly* tuned *flat*-out meltdown just at the mention of the flat! I was surrounded by a sea of flattening flats and I flat-out refused to believe the flats were a sell-out, making excuses, but as high and cocky as I was, I couldn't hide the spreadsheet of truth. Women wanted flats, and the sky-highs were too high.

I mark this as the day my world turned upside down and inside out. I no longer knew if there was a God. I refused to believe the focus group's flat feedback and went behind their unfocused flat backs, holding an after-hours clandestine meeting with twenty staff members to get to the heel of it.

'Girls! If you *had* to be a shoe for an entire day, which shoe would you be?'

Ten girls squealed, 'High-heeled sexy stilettos, *Alannah!*'

Ten girls said flatly, 'Flats. They're just more *comfortable*. Sorry, Alannah, please don't hate us!'

Don't hate us?! For *flat's* sake, the ten flats wearers needed lobotomies and brand-new feet – the kind that could wear sky-highs!

I thought I knew what women wanted. Sky-high heels to go with their Alannah Hill ornamental outfits, not depressing flats *'for comfort, Alannah!'*

The ballet flats versus killer heels war raged in the nerve centre at Factory X for weeks. I stood tall on my high moral ground, while the focus group stood flat and short in a moral ditch, until finally, in an act of good will, I compromised and dutifully agreed to seven pairs of sky-highs and three pairs of flats. I was high-heelin' it to hell! I knew they were wasting their money and the flats wouldn't sell. *Burn your money, you'll see!* I thought to my smug sky-high self.

I called them flatterinas, flat to the ground with a teeny-weeny incy-wincy 1-centimetre heel. Actually, I wouldn't even call it a heel, more of a bend where a heel *should* have been. To shut me up, the focus group said I could have an embellished emerald stone on the front of the flatterinas.

When the 'Are You Getting Married?' shoe collection finally arrived in the warehouse, I helped unload the hundreds of boxes and then scissored the boxes open until I found …

Utopia!

The Cinderella glass sky-highs glowed like tiny chandeliers, gently sleeping in layers of tissue, while the *inhumane* fattening flats lay wide awake in their paper coffins, the embellished jewel too ashamed to shine. No customer in their right mind would wear a pair of those flat horrors, but every customer in their *right* mind would wear my chandelier glass sky-highs. I waved the shoes out the warehouse door, knowing the flats would end up dead in a Clear iT store. You wouldn't be able to *give* them away.

The chandelier sky-highs had no idea their tiny glass hearts were about to shatter. I wished someone had captured the smug 'I'll show you all, just wait and see' look all over my flat little face. Running with scissors in a pair of velvet sky-highs, I almost scissored a clog wearer from Gorman* on my way to get the shoe spreadsheet results.

Look at her twirl in her ballet flats …

Look at *me* hurl in your ballet flats!

I flat-out *refused* to believe the spreadsheet results, despite knowing most of the girls working in the bow teeks** had ditched their sky-high heels and were flapping about on the shop floor in flatterinas.

The flatterinas were the number-one bestseller, with the killer heel coming in tenth. A killer *tenth*!

I should have gone straight to hospital with a shoe-stress heart attack, but instead I argued with the focus group spokesperson.

'I don't believe that spreadsheet. Are you SURE? Absolutely one hundred per cent sure?'

'Spreadsheets don't lie, Alannah.'

'What would you know? You're wearing flats,' I said flatly. 'Killer heels are designed to slow a woman down … it gives people more time to admire our strength, poise and presence as

---

* The Gorman brand had recently been purchased by Factory X, which meant Gorman's clog-wearing staff were suddenly very close to my million-dollar turf! A long white curtain was hung to separate the Alannah Hill and Gorman brands, but a long white curtain couldn't make anybody feel 'separate', let alone somebody like me! Besides, the long white curtain wasn't soundproof, nor, as it turns out, clog-proof.

** A bow teek is the Alannah way of saying 'boutique'. It's more elegant. And romantic. And enthralling, and even a little galling! With a bow on top!

we swank past. You can't swank in a flat! Do you know it was a man who really made the high heel hot? A ponced-up bloke called King Louis XIV swanned about in the seventeenth century wearing a white high heel with a red bow! The French even named the Louis heel after him!'

'Alannah, you're not a *proper* feminist,' she snapped back. 'Men are responsible for the design of women's shoes! You didn't know that, did you? And I don't care who wore them first! High heels are designed to slow us down, to tame fleeing, running women – what better way to root us to the ground?'

'Good point! Not bad!'

I didn't like the 'you're not a proper feminist' remark, but I had to give it to her in her canary-yellow flats with her toes bulging out the sides. High heels could *possibly* be viewed as a symbol of oppression (although Louis XIV wore his heels until the day he died).

With the stats in, I had to learn to taper my love of the high heel to 6 centimetres, and sometimes even 4! I learnt what women wanted by listening to my customers' hearts, so I designed shoes with a Louis heel, a mule heel, a kitten heel, boots with a bow heel, and once, for a Valentine's special, I designed a floral gumboot!

I'm not too proud to admit I was wrong in my insistence that women only wanted to wear sky-high heels. I was incorrect again on the shoe of poverty after I noticed Gorman's bestselling shoe: the clog! There was no high-heelin' way I'd ever compromise and design a clodhopping wooden clog, but if I were ever *forced* to do so, mine would be made from Venetian glass with a detachable 14-centimetre killer heel. After I was finished with them, they wouldn't even resemble clogs, and I'd rename them clogaramas – for women with a killer instinct and a penchant for drama.

Women disguise our bad choices, disappointments and misconduct in our clothing, but in wearing flats, you can give the entire game away.

I'll always feel half-vulnerable and half-powerful in my sky-highs. A high heel *does* elongate your leg, and makes you feel like a demigod while you singlehandedly take on the world. In my Sunday best, the flat will *always* make me feel dumpy, frumpy, lumpy and grumpy.

And so, ladies, the next time you're unsure of a person, cast a judgemental eye over their shoes, and it will tell you everything you need to know about who they are, and will perhaps shed some insight into who they *really* want to be.

You're *not* a prancing ballerina just because you wear a ballet flat, and you're *not* a gardener just because you wear a gumboot, you're not a runner because you wear Nikes, and you're *not* a rock god because you wear a cowboy heel, and you're definitely not Louis XIV because you wear a Louis heel.

You have to *believe* in your shoe of choice. If you're a yes to a ballet flat, commit to that, but if you're a no to a sky-high, maybe it's time to give them a little try? Always remember, if you *think* you can't walk in high heels, you probably can't … you've given up too easily, and already lost the battle. And if you think you can *only* walk in high heels, the battle of the bunion is just beginning.

The blessing gown of *silent sadness*

Sometimes, I don't leave my apartment for four days and four nights. I lose all desire to step outside or communicate with the outside world (I make an exception for an Uber Eats delivery or a stand-off with a nosy neighbour). I call it the silent sadness.

The silent sadness is going to work and falling apart when you get home; it's making jokes so other people can't see you're the only one not laughing; it's texting *Sorry. I can't get rid of this damned stomach ache … let's reschedule?* (with an emoji for vomiting); it's faking smiles at social events when you've been fantasising about your own funeral – what colour coffin, what kind of music and who will or won't be permitted into the crowded church while Elton John sings 'Goodbye Norma Jean' (not dissimilar to Princess Diana's sad, sad funeral day). Sadness is silent because we are alone.

I have always spent much of my time alone. Being alone, for me, means a quiet place where demons and angels swarm and mini Magnums are consumed in bulk. Being alone means complete silence in complete solitude. No talking, no pleasure, no anything, because *everything* freezes my heart. I need the aloneness to weather the storm. Solitude: the constant companion clasping my hands.

Sometimes, in the absence of noise, we can find a remedy for our blues.

But there are times when the squid-ink clouds of gloom darkening my sky morph into thunder clouds, threatening a Nervy B*. After various near-fatal incidents, I now load my imaginary Smith & Wesson gun with blanks. Firing bullets is not healing, and the *bang bang bang* is not peaceful – I hate guns, but they're a great metaphor for the murderous feeling I get when the silent sadness darkens my world.

Often, it's the smallest of things that start my doomsday clock countdown. Four or more trivial occurrences in the one day can create an earthquake in my deepest oceanic depths, leading to a tsunami of negative emotion erupting like Mt Etna, a roaring, fiery trail of red hot ash and lava beckoning me to bask in its fiery emotional cauldron.

Dramatique!

Triggered depression is often invisible, and we try to carry on, hoping we can hide it. We try to hide it by *becoming* invisible. It's really difficult to live an invisible life even if we *feel* invisible and paper thin.

The triggers themselves can seem innocuous and petty – the kind of things you would barely notice on a different day. When the storm clouds settle I'm often left speechless by just how petty my triggers are. A spat with my son, an image of my mum, finding an Alannah Hill cardigan in an op shop, a funeral procession, a wedding procession, a pregnant woman with a loving husband,

---

* My mum's way of saying 'nervous breakdown'.

a fight with an energy provider, a random encounter with a joyful Alannah Hill fan, Christmas Eve, Christmas Day, Boxing Day, feeling ugly and worthless, my birthday … look at me go! My pettiness has no limits!

I could list 110 more triggers, but we'd be here for eternity. I've learnt to recognise and shy away from the big guns – the triggers that cause week-long hibernations. For example, I wouldn't *dream* of attending a dinner party, or an afterparty, or a botox party in Wonthaggi, and you couldn't *pay* me to go anywhere near the Melbourne Cup.

In the hour when we're most alone, all the love in the world isn't enough to fill our empty bathtubs. When the blues descend, and I feel the storm gathering momentum, I lock all the doors and pull down the shades so I don't inflict my storm on others. My nan used to say that nobody wants you when you're down, so I learnt to close myself off and revel in my own misery.

Revelling in your own misery is a thankless task – time loses all meaning and your thoughts spiral into a miserable, bottomless hole. When I'm deep inside the revelling, I worry that I'll never recover, that I'll be gloomy and bottomless and stuck in a hole for eternity, if forever isn't long enough. My misery only loves my own company.

My hair is limp and stringy and refuses to tease no matter how hard I backcomb, my eyes are too close together, and my head the size of an apple. I simply cannot function.

The thought of engaging with anybody in a meaningful, respectable way is a mountain too high to climb. I fear what might come out of my tight, mean, depressed little mouth! It's safer for *all* concerned if I stay indoors and sweep my blues away. The safety and quietness of my locked-down apartment is calling me with a Leonard Cohen tune and a really sad video to match. I know how to prepare myself for the onslaught of the blues – it's hibernation.

The symptoms of impending hibernation are easily detected. First, a constant feeling of restlessness and rage. The second symptom can become a little more dangerous for some: the absence of pleasure.

In the absence of pleasure, some people fall into a four-month coma. It can hoodwink you into withering away off the grid in a small country town, or back home with your parents. I think it's the reason why so many people adore dogs and spend $60K on dog chemo. These people have it sorted – they know when they get home, *somebody* is pleased to see them.

And so I prepare …

I fill the freezer with mini Magnums, Ingham's chicken tenders and Birds Eye Fish Fingers. I buy Coles gourmet pizzas, dips that I'll never dip anything into, cleaning agents (Jif and Windex mainly), fresh bread, seventeen chocolate bars, crumpets (they go mouldy and are never eaten but still I purchase them), Maggi noodles, a large jar of Polish pickles, fresh raspberries and one inedible, bruised avocado. I don't know why I bother with the bruised avocado. I don't even like avocados.

I announce to Ed and Hugo that I need to regroup, that I might be withdrawn and quiet. They understand, and God help them if they don't!

I need a few other things to help me recover from the blues.

1. CNN on 24/7
2. Netflix
3. A candle (the perfume must be gardenia, lavender, rose or a mixture of all three)
4. Leonard Cohen (the best of Leonard on shuffle)
5. Avoidance of all bow teeks, stores, supermarkets, 7-Elevens, primary schools, and all social media
6. A journal
7. No answering the phone or the door (except for Uber Eats)
8. Someone to blame for my current mood
9. A blessing gown of depression

If you haven't got a blessing gown, get yourself one immediately – it will help you count your blessings as you quietly recover. I don't think the blessing gown is given enough credit. Cold? Pop on a blessing gown. Distressed? Pop on a blessing gown. Feeling fat and frumpy? Pop on a blessing gown – it can hide a multitude of sins. Life falling apart? A blessing gown can fix that!

My real cure for the blues? A full domestic trifecta of sweeping, mopping and vacuum cleaning. What to do when the house is clean and my heart is still empty? An overdose of Netflix and a good stickybeak into other people's business from the safety of my hibernation.

Cured! That is, until the next bullet passes through.

I don't always see the bullets coming, but I hear the *bang bang bang*!

Late in 2019, I was blithely driving along Chapel Street, my thoughts a million miles away. Something caught my eye – or rather, the absence of a certain something caught my eye. My original bow teek, my first-ever retail store and the true home of my old label, had vanished into thin air! *Empty.* Gutted. A shell. Dead. My name was the only thing you could see – Alannah Hill, spelt out in sloping, handwritten letters. I nearly rammed three Japanese tourists in my Batmobile by accident! My heart, my soul, my everything had been inextricably entwined in that store, and despite being a know-all on my own feelings, I wasn't prepared for what happened inside my heart.

Utter devastation.

I drove home in a quiet rage, knowing I'd hurl myself down into a dungeon with no key to work through the grief of losing my identity *all over again.*

With trembling, freckled fingers, I reached for my blessing gown of silent sadness. I lit a candle, sobbed over the lyrics to Leonard's 'The Goal' and swept the entire apartment, including the back stairs, the front stairs and half of Robe Street, with CNN on repeat.

I couldn't sleep. I couldn't eat. I was cata-toxic! I was *furious* and dismayed at not being able to stomp out the grief despite popping on the blessing gown.

I decided to run away.

Where better to run than to Florence, Italy? *Perfect.* No reminders in Florence of my once-glittering career. No reminders of my shell-shocked bow teek. Hugo was on tour in

Italy* and on a whim and a nightmare, I flew like a sequin to Italia. I could fit into Hugo's schedule – I'd entertain myself while he was working. I'd be paperback writing, and I loved being alone. I needed aloneness. But I forgot something. I clean forgot that *you take yourself wherever you go.*

I'll repeat that. *You take yourself wherever you go.*

On my sixth day in Italy, a kind lady sent me a photo of the shell of my once shining bow teek. She told me how outrageous it was. She posted it on Facebook and I followed suit, reposting her image and puffing up with pride at all the messages of love and support. Apparently, I was an icon, a true survivor, loved, adored – 'You're so inspirational, Alannah!'

Ahhhh, the comfort of strangers. I felt hugged and loved, understood and respected. I *was* Florence Nightingale in a glorious Florence residence. And yet, in the faraway distance, I sensed the darkening clouds gathering with sudden, violent discharges of high-voltage electricity. A bad moon was on the rise …

I'd been writing all day, penthouse high, with glorious views that would make a storm cloud weep, each window a picture postcard of Renaissance light, the Duomo like the Garden of Eden. I'd written until I had no more words to give. I'd lost my heated hair rollers and my hair was flat! No volume, no vim! I needed to buy a new rolling set, so I Florenced myself up in a polka-dot dress and stepped out onto the streets to bask in the

---

* Hugo is a musician and producer, and he tours around the world *four* months of the year! Italy is his second home!

glow of the magic hour. My God, I looked like Sophia Loren! Or maybe even Mary Magdalene. I'd covered my head in a French lace scarf, and had on my black Tom Ford sunglasses and sherbet-bomb lipstick. There were people everywhere, ratty tourists, families, fun-loving couples, crying babies and one lone priest.

'I'm in Florence, I'm in Florence … who cares about that shell of a shop! I'm an Aussie icon … la de la de la … de-la-eeeeluded,' I sang to myself on the Ponte Vecchio bridge after purchasing a leather tote bag that I didn't even like.

Nearby I could see storefronts of the world-dominating brands: Prada, D&G, Miu Miu, Chanel and Christian Dior. I had no intention of buying anything. I was just looking at their 'fit-outs' and how the staff all wore white gloves and how I couldn't afford to buy anything. I was jealous they weren't shells … and their fit-outs were exactly what I imagined for myself. I tried on a Prada skirt, deep red and floral with a black velvet ribbon. It was pure perfection!

'*Combien?*' I asked in perfect French. The clouds were moving fast and my Italian was letting me down.

'*Combien?*' the Italian assistant repeated. '*Combien?*' (She said it twice because she knew I was a little off colour.)

'Yes! *Combien!*' I snapped back. '*Com-beeee-EN!*'

'Four thousand and eighty-nine euro.'

Really? You're joking, I thought to my invisible self.

I nodded along with the sales assistant in her white gloves with her perfect fit-out. We nodded and blinked, and acted as though it was completely normal for a skirt with a velvet ribbon to be basically $6500. My eyes locked into her blinking blue eyes and I imagined saying, 'I could make that for four hundred and fifty-nine dollars. I could even make a better version! The buttons are quite loose on the back of that skirt and the velvet ribbon, well, it's not the *best* quality velvet ribbon I've ever seen. And who the hell is going to pay six and a half thousand dollars for a skirt with inferior velvet ribbon? You're *dreamin'*!'

The storm clouds were gathering force. I bought that skirt (and returned it the very next day). Next I stumbled across a jewellery bow teek. I needed a new necklace, and so I tried one on. Shiny black pearls around my neck. My God, I looked like a movie star! I *was* Sophia Loren! I tried on four more. I felt so good I bought them all, and wore them out of the store. Before I'd crossed the next piazza, I'd forgotten I was wearing the necklaces of contentment.

Because you take yourself wherever you go …

I had to get back to my Florentine residence. The families, the posh bow teeks, what was I thinking? I needed to *hibernate*. But how? I had no blessing gown, no candle, no Leonard Cohen, no broom, nothing to sweep, no CNN, no Netflix. I threw myself into a busy restaurant on a crowded Florentine street. I couldn't speak. I couldn't order any food. I pointed at the pasta menu and the waiter brought me an entire fish. I don't like fish. I ate the free bread and then hid in a side street. Four Italian lads eyed me as I walked toward another piazza. One of them held out a clear plastic bag with a pink pill dying inside and casually asked for €50. Fifty euro?

'Give to us fifty euro … give it … *give it now*,' he said in broken English.

I thought about it. *I did!* I thought about buying that hot-pink pill. I wondered if it might help. Maybe it would even bring some comfort! The Italian lads were smart. They knew they'd caught me off guard. They closed in for their fifty. Then I heard my voice shouting '*Vaffanculo!*'*

And they fled, fled for fear of their druggy little lives.

I staggered on past Dior, had a panic attack outside Chanel, sobbed at a loving family and winced at the overwhelming vision of the Duomo lit up by a full moon. The clouds were out in force. The entire city of Florence was slipping and dipping like a giant, medieval cruise liner tossed on the waves of my silent sadness. Like Bambi straying into crossfire, I was out on the streets. Splintering in my mind, bombshell fragments and shrapnel grazed all I held dear – my past, my dreams, my brilliant career, all burnt up in black smoke. I wondered how the hell I was going to put out the fire. With water or a blessing gown or both?

Limping past Hermès, I said a silent prayer to Saint Anthony. My mum always prayed to Saint Anthony. She thought he cured 'heartache', but in real life Anthony was the Patron Saint of all things lost and found. (No wonder my mum was so heartbroken. She'd been praying to the wrong saint and never found what she had lost.) I stared up at the glowering heavens, hoping for an answer.

Through the clouds I saw temporary salvation. I couldn't believe it, but right in front of me stood a lost and found store – and when you're a lapsed Catholic, you'd swear on the Bible

---

* I'd learnt one swear word: it means 'eff off' in Italian.

it was Saint Anthony who'd found it. The lost store was a candle store, a blessing-gown store, a music store and a candy-bar store. I purchased all my little comforts on my credit card and I pushed on, turning in circles, past more bow teeks, more people …

My trigger finger was getting twitchy. I really needed to get back to my smashing little residence and sweep. Number 18 on the Via del Corso – the lift flew me up but I stopped it on the third level. I'd spied a housekeeping room two days earlier and I knew there'd be a broom hiding inside. And there it was! What a find! What luck! The broomstick was waiting for me. I slipped into my blessing gown, Leonard sang me 'The Goal' and I swept! I swept Florence with such fury, I feared for the broom. I swept the one hundred steps, the long grand hallway. I swept a public bathroom, my residence and an entire empty apartment. Nobody noticed, but I swept my blues and the shell of 'what once was' into the Florentine streets …

Until the next time.

How do we let go of the blues? How do we let go of our negativities and deep hurts? A blessing gown of silent sadness can bandaid our blues, but when we lay our heads down on our pillows at night, the room shrinks and the temperature drops, and it's in these darkest hours we lie wide awake, daring to imagine a different life or fearing the one we have.

So stop procrastinating, slip off your blessing gowns and put your best foot forward! Colour your lips cherry red, slam a few doors and get out amongst it, because where you stumble is where you'll find your treasure ...

There will be fear.

There will be failure.

It takes a lot of nerve, a lot of courage, a lot of digging to change familiar patterns of behaviour. I'm all for a change in location to help put things right – a weekend away, a holiday in Italy – but no matter how invisible you think you are ... the storm clouds you're running from will find you, wherever you go!

Postscript: Sadly there is no real cure for the blues. But for the moments in between, pick up a broom and sweep the blues away!

The bathing costume of *calamity*

I thought I was allergic to Bali.

I thought of Bali as a *beautifully* corrupted island full of acid casualties, end-of season football trips and functioning alcoholics. Overcrowded and over-polluted, with hungry, wild animals roaming every beach.

When I thought of Bali I saw boogie boards and people on the run, a place where you're thrown in jail for life for possessing a marijuana joint. A place where pristine beaches were ruined by hordes of untamed children digging sandcastles with life-sized moats and playing the worst game of all time: beach cricket. And nothing saddens me more than a person freshly returned from Bali with a full head of beaded cornrows: the Bo Derek. (People fresh back from Bali don't understand you *cannot* be Bo Derek just because you've got cornrows. You're still yourself, but with a really unflattering hairdo.) Bali was full of backpackers, drug smugglers, animal poachers, Russian mafia and Aussie tourists.

I didn't understand why anyone would go there.

So how did I come to wake up at the Legian luxury five-star resort in Seminyak with a panoramic view of the Indian Ocean and a vivid Bali sunrise? A resort complete with a state-of-the-art wellness centre, private plunge pools, kidney-shaped swimming pools and a butler for every king-sized suite.

Me, alone with a nine-year-old, a young woman called Cherry and an allergy to Bali.

When Ed told me he *desperately* wanted to visit the sacred monkey forest in Bali, I was mortified. When he told me he wanted to ride elephants in Bali, I told him it was cruel and the elephants really suffered. I asked him if he'd like someone riding around on his back all day and he said he'd love it. Saddle him up and he was ready to roll, he said. I told him that outside every home and shop hung tiny lampshade-sized cages housing birds that were throwing themselves against the bars in despair. And on the floor, lampshade-sized wicker cages with trapped cockerels sat in the hot sun, awaiting their evening fight to the death.

Nothing worked. He had friends who were going to Bali on their annual family holiday and he didn't want to miss out. 'Please, Mum? *Please?*'

'No, son, no! I told you, love, anything you want, but *no Bali.*' (Also no dogs, no drugs, no alcohol, no swearing and no leaving home. Ever.)

Don't get me wrong – I firmly believed every kid should have an annual family holiday. Ed's father, Karl, and I were happily co-parenting and, luckily for me, my sister was co-smothering right alongside me, so we had our own version of a family. A *faux* family.

In return for Karl helping me with Ed, I shouted him an annual faux-family trip away. Just the three of us! We both had new relationships, but we were co-parenting *together.* We had travelled to Thailand, Singapore, Tokyo and, once, due to my googling inexperience, we ended up on a remote resort in

Savusavu, Fiji. Once you were on the island you couldn't leave. The planes flew in from the main island just once a week. The island was spectacular, specialising in deep-sea diving, organic vegetables and a reducetarian diet (less meat, less fish, less dairy, less dessert). I loved dessert, but I couldn't get the chef to make me a pavlova. He didn't know what a pav was. Dessert was instead four fresh home-grown raspberries delicately placed on a huge white plate, with a dash of mint and icing sugar. (I cannot tell you how many plates of dessert I ate.) The rooms had unparalleled access to some of the world's most spectacular land and seascapes … but there was no television. I repeat, *no television*. And I had no interest in islands, diving, swimming *or* landscapes – I spent my time poncing about in glamorous island outfits, showing Karl what he'd missed out on.

Faux family life was truly exhausting.

But as it turned out, my googling inexperience turned out to be an experience of a lifetime. The faux-family island holiday was so spectacular we barely missed the television. We participated nicely in the island's social events and I even joined in the ritual of drinking kava. On the morning we left, the staff sang a Fijian goodbye song and it was so damned moving I stuffed down tears in the buggy to the airport.

In the end I caved in with Mother of the Year–level love for my son and booked our faux-family trip to Bali because I worried Ed wouldn't have any chums over the Christmas break. And as you know, there wasn't a thing I wouldn't do to make my baby son happy.*

---

* Love me forever!

Maybe I could commune with sacred wild monkeys and maybe I *could* climb on top of an elephant. I didn't have any interest in normal beach culture, but I did have my own version of poolside couture. My inner Bo Derek could emerge as I got my thin hair cornrowed. And sure, I'd have to mingle with normal families – I dreaded it, but I could pretend. For a week.

The day before we were meant to leave, Karl cancelled.

He was terribly sorry. Really, *really* sorry. He made the insane suggestion that I should take a friend instead. A friend? I was too busy becoming successful to cultivate healthy friendships. My faux friends worked at the Factory X office but I was well aware they were also double agents, part-time spies, working for the man.

A nanny wasn't an option. Apart from the impossibly short notice, I feared travelling with nannies. I'd never quite recovered from the nanny debacle in London and Paris when Ed was six months old. Plus, travelling with a nanny made me feel lonely. My sister couldn't go – for a start, she didn't even have a passport.

I was furiously hurt and, like all furiously hurt mothers, I used my child as leverage to ignite the flame of guilt in Karl. How could he do this to his son? To *me*? To *us*? I told him Ed was *really, really* looking forward to befriending the monkeys and climbing on top of elephants, and seeing the tiny birds who lived in lampshades. How could Karl do this to our *family*! (Imagine lots of crying and probably a shriek or two here from me at this point in the guilting.)

Karl then took it a step further and suggested I go solo with Ed. Just the two of us.

My stomach hit the floor. Forget about Bali belly, I had Bali body and I wasn't even there yet! He'd lost his mind. Me? A single mother? I reminded him that I had *important work* to do while I was away, that I couldn't be with Ed 24/7. How on earth could I manage alone with an indulged nine-year-old on a tawdry island for an entire week?

How?

I panicked and sweated and had calamitous thoughts. I'd never been alone with Edward for more than two or three days in a row. I wasn't a natural mother, and a week alone in Bali would surely reveal all my flaws, all the cracks in my maternal armour. I feared that I wouldn't be enough, that Ed would turn away when he discovered it was just me for seven sleeps. I couldn't go to Bali without Karl or my sister. It was ludicrous, and I quickly became riddled with critical doubts.

And then the quick-fixing side of me swung into action. Within twenty-four hours, Karl had been replaced by a young girl called Cherry. She was my best salesgirl in the Chapel Street bow teek and she loved kids – she'd even been to Bali. Instead of rostering her on for a week in the store, I rostered her on for a week in Bali. She was thrilled.

Cherry didn't complain about boredom on the six-hour flight. She played noughts and crosses with Ed while I flipped through pages of *Vogue Italia* with my heart racing and my doubts soaring. In the back of my mind I knew I hadn't really thought this through.

I planned to work on my winter collection, and *Vogue Italia* was helping me out. I hated a trend, and magazines gave me both inspiration and insight into what to avoid with the ghastly trend situation. I ripped out any page that took my fancy and some pages that didn't. I wanted Cherry to see how I could multitask and manage a high-flyin' fashion career on an aeroplane while being an adoring mother with my adored son. The more pages I ripped, the harder she'd think I was working.

Rip, rip, *rip*!

I was catastrophising about my complete inability to relax, and plagued with extreme doubts about whether I had the stamina to keep up the charade of being a staggeringly good mother. I tried hard to come across as a natural mother in public, but seven days at a resort … I didn't know *anyone* with that kind of stamina.

My doubts kept nagging and clawing at me when we arrived at the resort a little after 4 pm. It didn't help that I was squashed into a Bali golf buggy with eight suitcases, while trailing behind were Cherry and Ed in another buggy with six suitcases.

Our traditional dark-wood Balinese suites were each the size of a small suburb. My bed was king-sized with pure white Egyptian-cotton sheets. I had my own office, and a TV screen in the bathroom. There were sprawling leather sofas and panoramic views from every terrace. We even had an outdoor jacuzzi. My heart started to melt and I fluttered in the Balinese candlelight when I saw Ed's excited holiday face.

Breathless, Cherry bounced into my room, interrupting all my furtive doubts. She was *beside* herself. Did I know her room came with *two* butlers? Each one alarmingly more attractive than the other? No, no, I didn't know that, Cherry.

Cherry loved men. I'll repeat that: Cherry loved *all* men. Which is why I often had to remind her that she had terrible taste in men.

On our first Balinese evening, Cherry and I dressed up in vintage gowns and ordered room service. I didn't feel social enough for the hotel restaurant, so we sat with Ed on the perfect balcony chatting about the week ahead.

At this stage, it's important to note that I hadn't actually explained to Cherry what her role was in Bali, what I expected from her. A normal mother would have outlined the job description before handing her the ticket! But there was a bigger problem arising on the Balinese horizon.

I didn't have any boundaries. I didn't really know what they were, or how to get them. I wasn't sure what people meant when they talked about how they changed their lives by putting some hard-won boundaries in place.

Boundaries! The mere idea of a boundary made me feel hemmed in, controlled and restricted. I could usually see a line in the sand but even when I knew I wasn't meant to cross it, inevitably I did.

I had a vague idea that parenting books were big on boundaries. 'Are you saying yes when you should be saying no?' (I rarely said no.) But this seemed more relevant to normal mums than me, a trail-blazing, boundary-busting single mum.

To be perfectly frank, dear reader, I'm pretty sure that the brows of successful CEOs and entrepreneurs (myself included!) would furrow when grilled on the boundary situation. 'What's a boundary?' they'd ask. Our switched-on brains struggle to comprehend what boundaries are for. We never switch off. We're always on the job because we *are* the job.

I didn't need to be sitting at a computer to be working. I was thinking and looking and emailing and designing collections and organising fashion shoots in my head; my mind was busy 24/7. There were no boundaries between work and home for me. *No boundaries.*

Cherry wasn't to know that boundaries were one of my biggest weaknesses. She probably thought this sojourn in Bali was a reward for her outstandingly good shopgirl performance or for dibber-dobbing on the bow teek staff who had the gall to wear a flat! In my boundaryless universe, I assumed she would move from one high heel to the next, from shop floor to playground, from Chapel Street to Seminyak, as number-one confidante, nurse, best friend, trusted custodian, understudy, lady-in-waiting, *chiquita*, home girl, playmate, BFF, ex-husband and, if she had any time left, nanny.

We'd planned to meet at 11 the next morning so Cherry could sleep in. Mother of the Year over here had been up since 5.30 am cheating at Monopoly, playing Scrabble and saving my son from drowning. Thank the water gods I had the good sense to strap his arms inside floaties. But unbeknown to the six-year-old, I was on a Melbourne fashion deadline. I had to send my mood board through to Factory X asap for my upcoming winter collection (aptly named 'He'll Never Love You, Dear'). I was getting hot and bothered just thinking about my new colour: Bali Black.

I knocked gently on Cherry's door the next morning, once, twice and thrice.

Nothing!

Odd. I was sure I'd told her I had a mood board to complete. Hadn't I?

Ed was nagging me to be a normal mum, which seemed to involve diving head-first into one of the giant organ-shaped swimming pools. I don't know why five-star hotels are so quick to boast about their kidney-shaped pools. I was convinced you'd *lose* a kidney if you swam in a pool like that. If I designed a pool I'd make it heart-shaped.

But there was an even bigger problem arising on the new Balinese horizon. I couldn't swim. Ed thought he could, but I hadn't taken him to any swimming lessons. I hoped the school might have taught him.

Where the hell was Cherry?

Ed was onto it pretty quickly. It was just him and me. And I wasn't going to be enough.

'Ed! I have to work on my mood board, love. I promise I'll throw myself in the shark-infested waters when I find Cherry.'

'You're no fun. You call yourself a fun mum and you're not even any fun. Why did we even come? You're a bum mum!'

Where the hell *was Cherry?*

'Please, MUM. Get in the water with me? Just put on that dress you wear in the water and jump in.'

This is when I realised Cherry must have been kidnapped. All the signs were there – she wasn't answering her door and she appeared to be missing.

I told the police that I'd last seen Cherry wearing teeny-weeny cut-off denim shorts, a floral blouse loosely tied in a bow at her bellybutton, no bra and black high-heeled boots. I tried to explain to the police that you could buy a house with the money you could trade for Cherry's hair. She had *Vogue* hair. Long, wavy and chocolate brown. I urged the police to lock down all hairdressing salons, and demanded signs offering a reward for her return.

They didn't take a lot of notice of my urgings. They were too busy perving on the picture of Cherry I'd provided. She looked like a sixteen-year-old supermodel, tanned, sexy and wilful, like a milky *Cherry* Ripe!

Without Cherry I was alone in Bali with a nine-year-old and chronic disdain for the sun. And I had to pretend to go swimming because I'd do anything for my adorable son.

My waterside garb has been *mocked* and scorned around the world. I claim that wearing a loose floral frock to the beach or pool (and in the water) reduces stress, sunburn, freckles, upset, humiliation *and* severe wrinkling. The mocking, *jeering* and flat-out *beach bullying* over my remarkable beekeeping get-up (which doubled as a skin-cancer-prevention costume) whenever I appeared waterside anywhere was rife. I knew Bali would be no different.

Even though I was known to show off, I was also sensitively modest. The harsh sunlight wasn't kind to the flaunting of flesh, and I felt much prettier wearing a frock in the water. So in Bali, I tried to blend in with a floral dress, embellished sequined cardigan, a high heel, a fascinator with protective veiling, gloves for my hands so they didn't freckle and a flowing vintage throw … and enough make-up to sink the *Titanic*.

I found a shady spot on the beach where Ed and I could lie down on a white sofa bed and lose ourselves in the view. I was feeling guilty about not working, while wondering if Cherry was in the process of being chopped up. I didn't get away with peaceful view-gazing for long. I think all mothers know you don't get away with gazing when you've got children. (Except at school reports, and that's called double-gazing in horror!)

'Mum. Mum. *Mum.* Get in the water with me, *please?*'

I caved.

I hobbled toward the shoreline, beekeeper-style, holding Ed's hand a little too tightly. As suspected, the beach was a horrible fright. Cornrows by the thousands, children screaming, parents sleeping, paid nannies on phones and the air thick with the smell of coconut oil – everything to make a woman feel bilious.

A wave splashed on my body and I stuffed down a shriek. Ed seeming to be really enjoying himself and – being the excellent mother that I am – I kept him company. That is, until I couldn't take it anymore. I told Ed the water was swarming with sharks and they had a bloodthirsty taste for kids paddling near the shore. He turned into the Road Runner – I'd never seen him move so fast. He was happy to sit and watch for the imaginary sharks I occasionally pointed out in between *Vogue Italia* rips. Mother of the Year strikes again!

I wasn't doing so badly with Ed on my own, although I forgot that kids need a solid lunch and so when Ed wanted hot chips, I was more than happy to get them. I wasn't even thinking about my winter collection – I was thinking about sunscreen and how Ed's back was flaming red. I slip-slop-slapped sunscreen all over him and hand-fed him French fries. It was the least I could do after burning him to a crisp! And after the chips, the kiddies *always* want a drink. I was more than thrilled to show everybody at the beach how patient, kind and giving I was. I hoped they could see what a splendidly normal mother I was, getting up for the *second* time to get my son his lunchtime Fanta.

When I came back, Ed was gone.

Disappeared into the thin Balinese air.

All the blood left my body.

Kidnapped! Like Cherry!

At first my shrieking was quite dignified. 'Ed-*wood* – if you're hiding, come out now, will you, dar*ling*?'

And then I snapped. My baby talk became a giant lioness *roar*. I was thinking about Bali as the nerve centre for global organ theft.

A family from Ed's school found my son not far away on the tourist beach close to the gilded-cage five-star resort. And they let me have it: the normal mum told me Ed should have had a sign around his neck saying that he couldn't swim, and that perhaps instead of hand-feeding him French fries, I should teach him how to at least dog paddle.

Somewhere along the way my fascinator had become waterlogged, and a rivulet of what looked like pale-red blood was oozing from my head. I could see the mum eyeing it off, so I told her I was a fashion designer. I don't know why I thought that would help the situation – it only made it worse.

Edward had been found on the beach surrounded by shrewd hawkers and part-time gypsies with heavy bags on their tired backs, carrying scarves, thongs, tote bags, saucepans and hot-pink shell necklaces with hot-pink shell bracelets to match. Ed had at least five pairs of sunglasses on his head, and was complaining about the sand. He was having his feet massaged while another hawker draped myriad silk cloths over his face, demanding money. Ed had told them his mum would buy everything (because she was good like that).

And I *was* good like that!

I bought the lot.

The total cost of the beach hawkers' wares was $2K. I asked the hotel concierge to pack and ship it all to Factory X. I'm pretty sure the contents of the Bali beach package ended up in a Clear iT store on Brunswick Street.

Without Cherry, without my sister and without Karl, I was juggling a trifecta of roles!

Boundaryless Mum

Normal Mum

and

Entertainer Mum

My Entertainer Mum act was a real hit!

The very next day, I surprised all the kiddies by sneaking in through the gate of the Kids' Club with clanging pots and ordiments* from the hawkers on the beach. Or maybe I freaked them right out (I *was* like the Hare Krishnas). Clang, clang, clang, bash, bash, bash, clang, bash, bash, clang … A few kiddies screamed for their mothers or nannies but five minutes later they were *putty* in my hands. I told them I was Queen of the Underworld with a magic tail. My magic tail threw kiddies into

---

* Ordiments is the *correct* way of saying 'ornaments' (the odd little china things we collect along the way).

the pool, up beach slides and from side to side. I threw packets of lollies in the pool and whoever found a lolly immediately got ten more. The kiddies were pumped! Everybody joined in the madness at the Kids' Club and I like to think my visits gave the Balinese nannies a genuine break.

I still hated Bali, but entertaining kiddies made me feel like the happy mermaid!

Where the bloody hell is Cherry? had turned into *Whatever, Cherry Ripe.*

With no sign of Cherry, Ed and I had more room service, we dog-paddled in a glittery blue pool, we rode motorbikes, and we even visited the infamous Bali monkey zoo where sacred wild monkeys hang like hungry, mad bats in trees. They were known for attacking tourists so I found it rather odd that right outside the monkey zoo were two handwritten signs:

DO NOT FEED THE MONKEYS –
YOU MIGHT DIE
and
FEED THE MONKEYS –
ENTER AT OWN RISK

The second sign appealed to Boundaryless Mum, so I took the risk with Ed and we entered at our own risk with an armful of bananas. Ed made Alannah Banana jokes. I still don't quite know why the monkeys attacked us, but attack us they did! I blame it on a fellow who sidled up to me and asked if I was the famous ladyboy appearing at the new casino. Apparently, I looked just like him. Maybe it was my look of scorn that startled the monkeys, but suddenly Ed and I were thrown to the ground with monkey after monkey scratching and biting our backs and heads – and raiding the banana bag. Their crazy eyes bored through our skin and, being the lifesaving mother that I was, I threw myself fearlessly onto Ed's back, protecting him from certain death by monkey mauling.

On the fourth day, Cherry came back. She was really, *really, really* sorry, but wouldn't you know it? She'd fallen madly in love with the Balinese owner of a drycleaners. Ketut and Cherry were engaged! How bloody wonderful! They were planning a Balinese wedding! I wanted to give her a little slap. But I didn't. She was about to get a rude Balinese awakening. If it was the same drycleaner I knew of, he was already married!

I quietly took the Boundaryless Mum blame for not being straight with Cherry about her seven-day job description. And frankly, Cherry could have done with a few boundaries herself because she was a love addict. (She would have been a winning contestant on *Love Island*).

I could blame my own boundary-lacking childhood and rebellious, wicked ways for the boundary situation. But the very real reason I have trouble with boundaries is because I'm a scaredy cat! Too afraid to say what I want out loud for fear people will think I'm a boring or, even worse, *ordinary.*

When I finally dipped into a self-help parenting bible, I discovered that if you're serious about setting boundaries, you need to visualise an imaginary compass with a large *yes* and a *no*. This compass helps normal people make decisions throughout their lives. It's as simple as tuning in, letting the arrow spin and choosing yes or no. Well, my imaginary compass was blurred – impossible to read. I didn't have a boundary-hopping hope.

On our final night in Bali, Cherry and I drank sickly undrinkable cocktails. Edward wanted his own, but I was learning to say no! Cherry's tan was golden, and Ed's sunburn was a brilliant flaming red. We ordered fries to our separate garden hammocks and watched *Toy Story 2* on a giant movie screen with surround sound. We watched the moon slide above the horizon, lighting up the beach with a supernatural Balinese glow.

Cherry spotted a Brad Pitt lookalike loitering in the villa next to ours and, like a snow leopard, raced off to see if there was a wife. She promised she'd stay out of strife.

I didn't mind. It was her last night and her Balinese engagement was in tatters! Ketut was clingy and Cherry didn't like that. He was also married but she didn't know that. Given Cherry's terrible taste in men, I doubt the loiterer looked anything like Brad close up. With Cherry searching for Brad, a break in the clouds reminded me it was just Ed and me.

The two of us.

My heart melted when Ed fell out of his hammock and climbed up into mine. It nearly exploded when he said, 'I love you, fun bum' and fell asleep in my freckled arms. Just the two of us.

That was our last faux-family trip, because I learnt that I could be alone with Ed, with or without boundaries. Mother of the Balinese Year over here had a Balinese epiphany. I came to understand in Bali that I was enough.

Postscript: As the years pass, we discover new boundaries. We bump up against the rails as we make all our little mistakes. I designed new guardrails to keep me from careening right over the edge. But, dear reader, when it comes to mothering, there are no boundaries around my heart-shaped pool of blistering, sunburnt love.

The collar of
disdain

I used to have nightmares so terrifying, I feared going to sleep. In a lake filled with black oil, an old woman was trying to drown me. I was fast losing breath, and when I tried to scream, all that came from my mouth was ...

Woof! *Woof!* WOOF!

Yes, in my nightmares, I was a dog!

I hated dogs. I hated every single thing about them, filthy germ-ridden bombs of bad breath from decaying canine teeth. They stunk to high heaven. (Believe me, no perfume masks their smell.) I thought they were unpredictable, unsophisticated creatures.

I wasn't brought up with pets but after my father died, Mum went dog-mad and told me she'd *always* loved dogs. I didn't know what to think. For years, we'd ripped into Mum's neighbours' dogs and torn apart dog lovers and dog walkers. And as for show dogs? Forget it! They were inbred, pampered narcissists and their owners – unhinged! I thought they loved their best-in-show dogs more than their own children!

On a rare Christmas trip home to Tassie, I was astonished to find Mum serving cold chicken wearing a mangy fur collar around her neck. On closer inspection, the collar was a yappy, furry ball of tiny, vicious teeth and sharp claws. A dog. Mum with a dog?

I was outraged!

She told me she was lonely, and that she'd picked the fur collar up from a garage sale. She *loved* him! How could she? I felt betrayed – once a dog hater, always a dog hater. A leopard can't change their spots, and people can't change theirs – especially a dog hater, or so I thought …

Unfortunately, Patch became hooked on the nicotine from Mum's sixty cigarettes a day, went blind and died. I couldn't understand Mum's utter devastation. Patch's sacred ashes became the centrepiece of Mum's mantlepiece, taking pride of place in a velvet box.

Woof! *Woof!* WOOF!

One of the many things I hate about dogs is their *neediness*. I can't stand it! A needy glare from a dog is infuriating and their 'love me, *love* me love *me*' act didn't work on me. In fact, it made me turn the other way (and dare I say it, loathe them a little bit more).

I understand dogs can fill an emotional void. They're loyal and obedient, and if you're blind a dog can be a real help. But I was gobsmacked when a friend told me she allowed her labrador to sleep with her, *shocked* when another told me he'd spent $60K on dog chemotherapy! Why? Why not let the poor dog die in peace? Are you that lonely? Are you that insane?

I learnt to keep my disdain for dogs to myself. I knew I'd be judged as a cold-hearted replicant, unable to love, unable to give, and basically, just a really *cruel*, mean person who wasn't living her best life. (I hated the term 'best life'. How could anybody live their 'best life' with a dog yapping at their heels?) I recoiled (and was physically ill) after a friend's dog slobbered all over my new velvet skirt … and the blowback was harsh.

'*Why* don't you love dogs? You're missing out on life, and anyway, you don't *deserve* a dog's love. Dogs know who you *really* are. Don't you know a dog is man's best friend?'

I thought a dog was a girl's worst enemy.

My cat Tiddles was my great love and, besides, I knew those gun-totin' dog owners wouldn't appreciate my thoughts on dog training. I would encourage people to ignore signs like 'Dogs must be on a leash' and 'No dogs in this area', training owners how *not* to train your dog. But I also knew dogs needed a loving, doting family, not someone like me.

Dear reader, please don't get me wrong. I understand the power a cute puppy holds with their big eyes, clumsy bumblings and adorable faces. It's been scientifically proven that puppies (and babies) are designed to be cute, because a puppy isn't just for Christmas, it's a dog for life! (And if babies weren't cute, we'd never handle the screaming, pooping three-year-old tantrum throwers they evolve into on the way to becoming teenagers overnight.) Science has also proven oxytocin (the 'love hormone') goes up 300 per cent in the brain when a person gazes into their dog's eyes. And the scientists didn't stop there – 40 per cent of women studied said they receive more emotional support from their dogs than their partners! I couldn't believe it … and yet I could.

From the moment my son took his first breath I warned him, 'Anything you want, love, but no dogs … EVER!' I got away with that line for nine years until one fateful day when I was tricked into buying a beaglier pup for $1500.

I'd been lured into the Victoria Gardens pet shop by Ed and his dad, who seemed to be in puppy cahoots. It was already decided: Ed's dad, Karl, and I would share the chocolate-box pup so I'd only be *half* responsible.

But just as I was forking out the $1500 and Jack was being chipped for life, Ed's dad changed his mind. He said I could change my mind too … but being the love-struck mother that I was, how could I change my effing mind?

Ed was on the floor having a full-blown conniption, writhing in pain, the runt of the litter held close to his chest, screaming, '*Nooooooo* … he *chose* me to love him … and he's got a heart on his back! Mum, you *love* hearts … please?'

In my desperate need to end Ed's pain, I walked out of that pet shop with a $1500 beaglier pup.

Of course, we wouldn't be keeping him. I planned to return that doggie in the window the very next morning. I'd tell Ed that unfortunately the little pup was carrying a deadly beagle virus and his breath could kill with one viral bark.

As soon as we arrived home I turned into a raving lunatic and cleaning addict. Dog poo here, dog wee there, dog poo bloody everywhere! A Prada slipper torn to pieces, a Dior shoe heel nibbled, and fur everywhere! Jack bounced off the walls like a mad rubber ball, his tongue hanging loose like a cartoon dog's – he tore feathers from velvet cushions, chased Tiddles the cat away, and ate a pair of Yves St Laurent sky-high heels.

I couldn't wait to take him back to the pet shop. But I had luck on my side. The very next morning, little pup Jack made a run for the open gate and, *woof*, he disappeared.

I looked for him everywhere, but he'd vanished.

Woof! *Woof!* WOOF!

Problem solved.

Problem *not* solved.

I received a telephone call from a concerned dog-lovin'
stickybeak. He'd found Jack in his front yard and because Jack had
been chipped, lucky for me, he wouldn't *ever* get lost! I was furious.
I'd have to de-chip him. Then a huffy neighbour complained that
Jack's bark kept her awake at night, and suggested I get his voice
box removed. She was dead serious, and I'm ashamed to admit I
was mildly interested in the idea at first. A dog without a bark?
I'd never heard of such a thing!

Jack needed three walks a day so I tried wearing him out in
Fawkner Park. Set free, he'd bound off at the speed of light,
landing *inside* a family picnic. He'd scavenge food, frighten
children and then I'd disown him. Easy. I didn't *know* the stray
pup, I'd never clapped eyes on him. He wasn't mine! I didn't even
like dogs!

Jack couldn't be weeing and pooing inside at night and so I
locked him in the garage. I made him a bed on the warm leather
seats of my Batmobile but he refused to sleep, ate the leather seats
and barked like a litter of Satan's angels all night long.

Every morning for weeks I planned to take Jack the brat back,
but something always came up.

And damn, every single day that passed, Ed fell more in
love. He started insisting Jack sleep in his bed, because it was
cold outside.

Jack didn't like Pal so I fed him gourmet mince.

When the dog-hating neighbour insisted *again* that Jack's voice box must come out, I asked if she'd like *her* voice box taken out.

I started to feel guilty when Jack was left alone …

I started talking to Jack and asking his advice …

When I was blue I secretly cuddled up to him …

My boyfriend Hugo and I talked about Jack's feelings … all the time.

I realised that 'dog' backwards is 'God'.

I felt like an unfit mother if Jack wasn't fed and walked twice a day. When a dog lover told me Jack was fat, I told him *he* was the fat one and asked why he didn't like dogs!

And then I used the words 'therapy' and 'dog' in the same sentence …

What was happening to me? Was I under a super-galactic dog spell? I still had every intention of taking Jack back to the pet shop, but I was always too busy and, anyway, he wouldn't get in the car.

Then came the night that changed everything.

Jack woke me at midnight, barking mad, urging me with his face, tail and body to get downstairs. I ignored him. He didn't know what he was barking about. He was going back to the pet shop anyway.

He woke me *again* at 1 am, but this time his bark was more urgent. I thought I could smell gas. I didn't cook so I couldn't have left the gas on. The only way I could shut him up was to see what the hell he was barking about. I tripped down the red-carpeted stairs in my dressing gown, Jack's desperate barks guiding me outside into the garden and to the gas hot-water heater … something was not quite right. I definitely smelt gas. The pile of clothing I'd left to dry over the vent of the heater was *on fire!* The hot-water heater was about to *blow up!*

Instinctively, I turned off the gas, grabbed the hose and squirted those flames like a seasoned firefighter. I couldn't save the burning clothes, but I *did* save the house from being blown apart.

The plumber who later viewed the near-catastrophe told me if Jack hadn't woken me, the whole street would have blown up. There would have been nothing left but burnt-out craters where houses once stood.

Jack saved our lives that day. For a dog that seemed so daft, he'd shown an uncanny ability to smell danger, and for that I was forever grateful.

I can't say I've done a complete turnaround and adore all dogs. I'm still slightly disgusted when a dog slobbers all over me and that needy look *can* ruin my day, but I can say, honestly, I understand that dogs have a way of finding the people who need them. They fill a heart-shaped void we don't even know we have. Jack didn't just come into our dogless lives, he gave us a life.

I often stare at my collection of dog-ravaged Pradas and unwearable cardigans with their vintage buttons bitten off. I stare and marvel at how a $1500 beaglier puppy with a love heart on his back became part of our little family, central to our very existence.

Jack and I have been together for eight years now. He's one of my longest relationships. He sleeps on a pink cashmere blanket on my bed (because he doesn't like being alone). Jack comes everywhere with me, even Bunnings.

Perhaps, just perhaps, people can change their spots into hearts after all …

Woof! *Woof!* WOOF!

The
ball gown of
wrongness

There isn't a mum, aunty, nanny, carer, babysitter or grandmother who doesn't revel in a school scandal. People like to pretend they're *not* revelling but, let's be honest, *most* people *revel* in a good scandal; some are just better at hiding it.

I'd love to have the gift of pretending not to revel in a scandal. My Aunty Cecily (who for some reason took a dislike to me from the moment I was born) used to say I was picking Granny Smith apples in our orchard when God was giving out the gift of virtue. She said I got 'scandalmongering' instead of virtue.

Did you know that 'scandal' was originally a term meaning 'unseemly conduct in a religious person', especially if it encouraged a lapse of faith in another? Even that's a scandal! I knew religion would be involved in a scandal somehow – Aunty Cecily was the drunk nun from hell.

A good scandal allows us to temporarily cast aside our own ordinary lives, and a really, *really* good scandal can make a tired mother's entire week. A good scandal allows us to feel superior, and to judge until we faint … plus we get vicarious pleasure, all at the same time.

Scandalmongers!

I got caught up in a *terrific* scandal once at my son's primary school. I wasn't the ringleader and it wasn't just me involved (although I'm 100 per cent certain I got a lot more out of the scandal than others). The scandal remained a black mark against my name for years, and I feel it's one of the reasons that I wasn't permitted to attend school camps or given any extracurricular responsibilities.

The scandal went on for weeks and I was really disappointed when it was over. When the scandal was at fever pitch, I hoped the artist involved might give me a special deal on one of his photographs.

Bill Henson!

The internationally acclaimed photographer was *the* scandal (although I always thought the scandal was like a candle – it burned brightly for a few weeks and then the scandal blew out its own flame!).

Thousands of judgemental people who knew nothing about art had been insulted by Bill Henson's photography for years, and now the government had tried to censor it. All the prudes thought Bill's nudes were too rude. They were blasphemous, obscene images that disturbed the soul. War had been declared, a war of good art versus bad.

Sue Knight, the principal at Ed's primary school, was arty, strong-willed, progressive, loved kids and liked to take a risk. Sue took a big risk in 2008 and invited Bill Henson *inside* the school gates to search for a prepubescent kiddie to model in one of Bill's iconic photographs.

Bill seemed to prefer it if the girls looked like boys and the boys looked like girls, so there was a chance for everybody to be involved.

Parents were outraged. They didn't want their kiddies involved in blasphemous images. How dare Bill get inside the school gates and scout, they roared. Some parents were so angry they couldn't hide it, especially when they heard the chosen child model would be photographed in make-up with two horns attached to their head, their body semi-naked and wrapped in tree branches, sprinkled with blood and rose petals. I thought it all sounded rather interesting, especially with the branches and roses.

All media hell broke loose, from the left and the right!

The morning the scandal broke, it was as though the news crew was lying in wait just for me in all my politically incorrect glory. Maybe they'd heard that, under pressure, I was fond of blurting a good soundbite for the news cycle with my PINF problem:

Politically Incorrect No Filter.

I spun on my high heels and threw Ed up in the air when I saw the news crew. I hoped for everybody's sake my mouth wouldn't start running. You forget when you're talking to a reporter (perfectly made up with shining hair) that it's *not* just the two of you having a quiet chat about a scandal, but that the entire country is watching on.

As I swanked toward the waiting crew with my mouth in the shape of a cat's bottom, I overheard one of the Friends Of The School mums letting fly like a fembot.

'I don't send Bowie to school to be *objectified*, with his innocence lost. I send Bowie to school to learn how to *fly* ... to grow *wings* and create *rainbows* ... to be a *child* ... a doctor, a lawyer or a *dentist*! I'm *disappointed* in Sue Knight. I don't want to send Bowie to Melbourne Grammar but he can't learn to be a lawyer with strangers roaming freely inside the school grounds! Bowie had nightmares last night!'

Another mum, her kiddie's face covered with a paper bag, snapped to the news crew, 'Go away! I've got washing to do and who gives a stuff if some indulged kid models in a photograph. He'll get paid for it so eff OFF!'

(I loved this mum and later tried to find her. I thought we could be friends.)

When I arrived at the waiting microphones, unfortunately I *did* start over-talking in a melody of errors ...

'Am I *disappointed* in the school for allowing Bill Henson inside the school gates? Well, to be honest, love, the school gates are never locked. They're always open! See, they're nailed back, you couldn't close them even if you tried! A junkie came in last week and shot up in front of some kids, so technically, love, Bill just walked in because there *are* no gates. The school should look into that. I LOVE Bill Henson's work – I'd love to own a Bill but they cost *a fortune*! YES, yes ... I *am* disappointed in how the school's managing the scandal. My son is ab-so-lute-ly gorgeous. Here, I've got a picture of him on my iPhone. Look at him! He's young, wan and *totally* innocent. He's as white as a sheet and photographs beautifully. Do you know whose kiddie *was* chosen? Can you believe it wasn't my son? He's bitterly disappointed. The chosen child might get a big head and think they're the chosen one! Bill should have chosen *everyone*, then this drama wouldn't be happening!'

One of the judgemental mums took my arm and told the reporter I was 'just being theatrical'. She insisted my comments be ignored and that I wasn't to be taken seriously. She asked me if I'd *deliberately* missed the point, but I had immediately forgotten what the point was when I saw the microphone.

The Henson Scandal was the lead story all over the news that night. I was disappointed by the small grab they showed, but in that grab there was no other mum in sight! None! It was just me!

In the interview, I gave some arty advice to Bill, like painting a 'mother with her only son'. The news loop seemed to particularly like the part where I said I was disappointed that my son wasn't chosen. I briefly worried that the rampant editing made me appear a little shallow and I even briefly gave a hoot. I wondered about doing a short course in politically correct interviewing but in the next hoot I knew I'd fail miserably.

Sue Knight went on to shine her principled light all over another primary school on the other side of town. Most of the parents were really sorry to see Sue go. We all chipped in for her farewell and bought her enough flowers for her own funeral. (Unfortunately, my son wasn't chosen to give the funeral flowers at Sue's final school assembly.) Everybody cried. Sue Knight was a big loss, and I've heard on the grapevine the school has not been quite the same since she left.

The new principal had big shoes to fill, and a lot of parents felt something was awry immediately (it wasn't just me). She wore flat shoes and long skirts, had no hairdo and no make-up. Her voice didn't rise and it didn't fall. It was all a monotone, which is actually quite hard to achieve. 'Good morning, boys and girls and mums and dads ... isn't it a wondeeeeeeeer-foooool daaaaaaay todaaaaaay ...'

No. No. It wasn't a wonderful day today, and how dare she imply it could be! Most of us had been up with the birds squirting packet porridge down our kiddies' throats. And some had even been to the gym or baked a casserole and pretended they cared about their husband's day ahead, which is really exhausting when you're multitasking. And if you were like me, a single, working mum who had just received an email stating I had to start clocking in at 8.45 am from now for the rest of my life – there was no way you were going to have a wonderful day todaaaaaay!

One afternoon at the school gate I was handed an old-fashioned letter. It was marked PERSONAL. It was from the new principal.

This was it! I'd made it! A hand-addressed letter surely meant something big was about to happen. I'd had serious doubts about the new principal, but not anymore. She wanted to see meet at 3 pm sharp tomorrow. I planned to con her into allowing me to teach fashion design to Ed's class so I could see him playing in the sandpit and make sure he had friends. I couldn't wait!

I wore a pink ball gown to my meeting at 3 pm sharp. Waiting outside the new principal's office with a Diet Coke and a half-eaten Boston bun from Bakers Delight, I smoothed out the netting on my gown and triple-checked my high heels weren't covered in grass.

'Nice to meet you … *Alannah* … what *are* you wearing? Is that a *real* ball gown?' the principal asked.

'Of *course* it's a *real* ball gown, love!'

She didn't laugh, but I did.

The flats-wearing principal sat behind a small card table covered in papers, time sheets and stress balls. My ball gown and I sat stiffly on a black plastic chair and Ed's teacher, Stacey, sat on a white plastic chair. I had a sinking feeling this meeting wasn't about plaques for Alannah Hill, Patron Saint of Berserk Mothers.

The young teacher, looking anxious and tired, drew our attention to a child's drawing on the desk among the papers. Nobody spoke. You could have cut the air with a McDonald's meal deal. We stared at the drawing for at least thirty seconds until I broke the silence.

'Wow-EEEEE!! That's a terrific drawing, isn't it? Is this why I'm here? Has Ed won an award? I knew he was a genius!'

The air shifted.

'Take your *time*, Alannah. Look closely at your son's drawing. Are you really *looking* at it? Look into it. Is everything *all right* at home?'

(Of course everything wasn't all right at home. Was anything *ever* all right at *anyone's* home, I wanted to shout.)

The teacher and the principal explained how some of Ed's drawings were worrying … *very* worrying.

'How worrying?' I asked in a worried voice. 'I see nothing to be worried about? What's the worry?'

'Well, Alannah, this appears to be a picture of you and your son bathing together naked. What *is* all that foam all over Edward? Or is it … *cream?* And is that a *plum* or an *orange* floating in the bath? And is that a real *banana* on your head?'

'It's a *mandarin* in the bath! And the cream is Gillette *shaving* foam. Ed's drawn the banana very well, don't you think? If you *knew* how many cans of Gillette we go through a week, you would NOT believe it! I always put the *cans* in the right bin. I've studied what you can recycle.' (I had no more studied recycling than I'd studied a pair of flats. I was trying to prove I was PC.) 'I give Ed his daily fibre serve of fruit in the bath. We *have* to have a bath every night so I can make sure he eats his fruits, otherwise … well … he'd be … *fruitless!*'

'FRUITLESS!'

'Fruitless?'

'Yeah. Fruitless.'

'Alannah, we're not here to judge you' – they were – 'but can you see *anything*, well, how can I put it, a little lewd within the picture?'

'He's seven! At least he hasn't drawn me with a loaded gun!' I laughed.

'Do you have *guns* at home, Alannah?'

Good God, was she for real? As if I'd have a gun at home. (I didn't tell her about the Nerf gun – it was all the rage with the kiddies. It wasn't quite the right moment to let her know Ed and I fired polystyrene bullets at neighbours on a regular basis.)

Thing were getting a little serious and my powder was starting to run.

'Let's get *serious* here.'

(I told you! The principal was getting serious.)

'Your seven-year-old son has drawn you and him in a bath. He's drawn your breasts as two moons and has written "I luv

Mumz moons" across one moon – ahh, sorry, *breast* … Surely you understand why we at the school feel this drawing is a little *off*? I'm afraid it cannot be displayed at the Special Art Day next week. I'm sorry.'

My ball gown tightened, and my shoes slipped off my feet. This was a showdown, a takedown, a PC shakedown!

'I've got quite big breasts!' I shouted in a ladylike way. 'D cups! It's not my fault that to a seven-year-old they look like moons.'

And then I shoved Bill Henson's name in because I couldn't help it. 'What about Bill Henson? The gates are still open, you know! Any old junkie or stray dog can just waltz on in!'

They bristled, and I prickled. And then I spotted a diversion.

A photograph of Ed's teacher nursing a newborn baby with the Grade 6 teacher, Mandy, lay on the desk. A withered balloon bobbed expectantly in the air. The balloon read: *Congratulations Mandy and Stacey on your new baby girl.* They looked like two mothers with a newborn child.

I was confused. Where was the father?

In the back of my mind I knew I was on dangerous ground, but the intimate discussion of my bathing habits gave me licence to go personal; I forged ahead in all my PINF glory. Yes, that's Politically Incorrect No Filter. *No filter.*

'I didn't know you were pregnant, love?'

'I wasn't *pregnant*, Alannah,' said Stacey. 'You don't have to be pregnant to have a baby. We informed the children of our *exciting* news last week. Didn't you get the notice in the red folder?'

'Oh Ed throws ALL the notices *away*, love! How can I stop him doing that?'

And then my mouth gave way to a fluttering of words that I didn't seem able to hold back.

'I know! You *adopted*!'

'No. We did not adopt, Alannah.'

Not adopted. This was getting tricky! My mouth began frothing with more un-PC remarks.

'I KNOW – you *bought* a baby! Where from? Russia or China? I heard adopted children are really well behaved. I'm convinced *I'm* adopted!'

'That's Mandy, me and our new baby girl, Kale ... we're both over the moon.' Tears of happiness fell down Stacey's cheeks.

Over the moon? I thought. *Interesting* turn of phrase, especially under the circumstances.

'I had NO idea you were a lesbian, love. My lesbian gaydar is way out! And sperm ... do you mind me asking, love ... was the sperm a friend's or a *complete* stranger's? Did Mandy have to have sex with an actual real man, love? Do I *know* him?'

It was one of the Friends Of The School fathers for sure. That kind of selfless giving could only come from one of them. The donor probably invented a PC way to deliver the sperm hidden inside a kale milkshake ...

A hollow silence filled the room. I was shocked and hurt by their suspicions about Ed's picture. I thought I was being singled out because of my dreary old past and I worried they were worried I wasn't able to manage my son.

'Loves ... imagine you're in the bath with little baby Kale. She loves soap and you love soap too ... you love soaping her up because they're your special soapy memories: moments in time that you *know* deep in your heart last only a split second. The little soapy versions of your child fly past like soap on a rope, soapy moments you won't feel ever again. Her lovestruck eyes will change colour and she'll gently turn away from you. You won't remember to say goodbye to all the little faces of baby Kale, because you won't notice her growing and changing. Time slows and speeds up and before you know it, baby Kale won't want to bathe with you. She'll tell you that you smell and to get out of her bathroom!

'And you will cry.

'And you will cry some more.

'And you won't know what to do. And you'll hold on because you'd do anything for one last bath. You're a mother now, love, so get ready for a lot of crying – you'll *never* get those lost moments back. Imagine when you are not the sun around which they spin. Imagine when they naturally grow apart from you and cast you aside like a safety pin. And, loves, don't you think the world's gone overboard with this whole PC thing? We're better than this, aren't we, loves?'

But my trump card was still to come.

'I could design baby Kale a dress. No gender, no colour? Or maybe ... a pink embellished ball gown?'

They both inched toward me, their eyes filled with tears. The ill-fated drawing blew itself off the desk when we all agreed that a pink embellished ball gown (with hessian booties) would be *absolutely* marvellous.

It was a moving moment in that little PC room of ball gown terror. I had to let them know there was nothing wrong or *off* with Ed's drawing. And I had to remind myself that *love* is what brings everything together – nuclear families, single-mum families, relationships, spirituality, metaphysics, lesbians, robots, gays (I'm on a roll) … who gives a flying moon?

Everyone has different values and no two families are the same. No matter how we try to conform to other people's ideas of who we should be, in the end we're only ever able to be the one self, our true self … with all our un-PC dignity.

For the record, I was also called in to the principal's office for one thing or another when Ed was in grades 4, 5 and 6, and years 7, 8, 9, 10, 11 and 12.

And when our children have all grown up, we grieve for their baby faces, their undying love and our memories in the bath.

I miss the time at primary school.

I miss the time being so uncool.

I miss the kids' faces

And silent empty spaces.

I miss not conforming

And my carry-on performing.

I miss the innocence.

I miss the past.

I miss the scandals.

But mostly, I miss my little boy blowing bubbles in the bath, because it all flies past so very, very fast.

The runner of *dissent*

I'm the type of person who used to imagine that I'd disappear into thin air and vanish for eternity if I was ever insane enough to step out in a casual runner (or *sneaker*). I worried that I'd lose my bloom, fall off my glittery stilts and drift away. I'd lose part of myself and become ordinary, vapid, wishy-washy, cold-hearted and really, really short.

A full-time casual runner wearer has little regard for human life and a lot of regard for animal life. They're fast and dominating and into armed robberies. Their life goal is to become an Instagram influencer. They have *no* idea about 'interior decorating' and brag about their 'interesting famous friends' when they don't have *any* interesting famous friends. They take really long showers and have no concept of time. They use liquid soap as opposed to a real cake of soap and sport 'casual' breezy hairdos.

A person would be hard-pressed to find a single casual thing about me, so naturally it was normal for me to catastrophise about disappearing into thin air. My entire world relied on not being casual and the thought of losing control in public was *astonishing*. I thought being casual would allow people to see through my careful construct of doll parts.

If people saw me in a runner, I worried they'd think I was an *international* tennis star, or glammed-up personal trainer running blindly around the Botanical Gardens with an easy-to-manage casual hairdo. They might even be tricked into thinking I held a tranquil, agreeable disposition, was fast on my feet, and said breezy things like '*C'est la vie*'.

I'd *never* say things like that. I had no idea if I was fast on my feet, and I certainly didn't have a sunny disposition. I'd never run around Luxembourg Gardens in Paris let alone a botanical one in Melbourne. And I didn't have an easy-to-manage hairdo – my hair was *impossible* to manage, really thin and there wasn't much of it.

I blame my deep-seated fear of the casual for my rebellion against a purpose-built shoe like the runner.

A dramatic podiatrist shocked my sensibilities after I was struck with an elderly person's problem – ingrown toenails. As I hobbled into the surgery, I blamed the ingrowns on my Tassie-girl genes and out-of-date nail varnish. Dr Scholl put his hand on my ankle and asked me to move my *talus* bone. I told him I didn't have a talus bone, but he assured me everybody did. He explained that, when we don't use our feet properly, our muscles have to strain to compensate – not just in our feet but in our whole body. He told me to stand on my tippy toes and to 'trust my bones to hold me up'.

And I have to tell you, in the bright glare of his stark rooms it felt like I had never stood up properly on my own two feet in my entire life!

He delivered the devastating news that if I continued to wear sky-high heels, I'd spend my twilight years in a wheelchair or, worse still, in a wheelchair wearing *Dr Scholls*.

He made grand assertions about high heels being linked to emotional pain, and argued high-heeling women like me had been angry for decades. He'd even written a paper called 'High Heels Make Women Angry'.

It made me angry when he printed it out and handed me a copy with an attachment named 'Hammer Toe'.

Have you heard of hammer toes? Don't despair, I hadn't either! Dr Scholl told me hammer toe is excruciating! It's caused by an abnormal joint forcing the normally flat toe to point downward … like a hammer! Bunions, corns and tight high heels all contribute to this repellent affliction. Dr Scholl wasn't interested in my ingrown. He was convinced that one of my toes was heading toward being hammered. He gave me a desperate warning about high heels and suggested the impossible – Dr Scholls!

I nearly poured my bottle of lemonade all over him but I didn't. I'm really restrained like that!

Dr Scholl didn't know the miles I'd travelled in my shoes. He didn't know I'd been pounding pavements in Harajuku and Shibuya on fashion buying trips for years, wearing 14-centimetre Dolce & Gabbana heels with no sign of a hammer toe. I was planning to pound those Japanese pavements again in a month's time. When old Dr Scholl made a last-ditch effort to sell me a pair of authentic Dr Scholl's sitting in a beige box in a tiny, dusty front room, I couldn't limp out of that podiatrist's fast enough.

One month later, in my luxe, expansive Tokyo hotel room, my pounding feet refused to be forced inside yesterday's 12-centimetre heels. That's right – *refused*! I tried shoving them in but both feet were swollen; some might even say *puffed up*.

I had ten hours of serious pounding of pavements ahead. I couldn't be wasting time with this puffed-up nonsense! I looked closely and there was no denying it. One toe *did* appear to be bent forward and *both* feet were crooked, and one was bigger than the other. Hammer toe? I seemed to have acquired a personal collection of hardcore bunions, searing corns and blistering red blisters … and now the swelling in my legs, bottom, calves and even my *hands* was puffing me right up. I couldn't find my little toes – they had both caved in on themselves and looked like two angry red M&Ms. My heels must have inadvertently eaten the toenails off, for they too had disappeared.

Dr Hill to the rescue!

I carried a foot first-aid kit when I was working, *just in case*. It was compact enough to hold a single bandage and five packets of gaudy Hello Kitty bandaids. A couple of Hello Kittys could mask a bit of blister pain, and five packets of the Kittys could mask corn *and* bunion pain. But I'd never had puffing before.

I tried shovelling my puffed-up Hello Kitty feet into the sky-highs again.

More rebellious, cowardly behaviour from my feet, refusing to be shovelled, and the packet of pretty Hello Kittys did nothing to reduce the swelling.

Ever resourceful, I tried dangling my puffed-up feet inside the hotel toilet bowl. I was hoping the relief from the flushing toilet would be instantaneous, that the cool water in the toilet bowl would literally flush my burning foot pain clean away.

Flushing didn't work. I almost called reception to ask what was wrong with the toilet – I was fast running out of options.

I thought I had power in a high heel, but they were now my Achilles heel! The only other footwear I had with me was a pair of Louis Vuitton 14-centimetre platforms with a half-eaten ankle strap (courtesy of Jack the dog). I couldn't shove my vanilla soufflé puffed-up feet into a Louis, so I did what any normal woman in a posh hotel room with two hot chilli peppers for feet would do. I slipped into the plush white hotel slippers.

Those slippers welcomed my Hello Kitty feet, hugging my shrunken toes, which uncurled and unfolded until they went into shock (they had *no* idea they could stretch out so far). Suddenly, I felt my mood spark right up; my face felt softer, and my pinched angry look … *completely* gone! Had I been in a fuming angry mood for most of my adult life because of heels? Here I was, flat to the ground, and I'd never been more comfortable and un-angry in all my life!

That's correct! Even the mere thought of flat footwear usually made me feel *flat*.

And that's how I came to wear white hotel slippers to a Nike bow teek in Shibuya with *this* mantra running through my mind: *A truly great casual runner is hard to find, difficult to part with and impossible to forget.*

Holding my first pair of casual runners, I clipped the hotel slippers onto my fascinator for a lark. I wish you could have seen the beaming smiles on the Nike staff's faces.

'Kawaii, *Kawaii!*' they squealed. (*Kawaii* means 'cute' in Japanese.)

And so it came to pass that I bought my first pair of runners in a Nike bow teek in Shibuya with a pair of slippers on my head!

And lo and behold, I *didn't* disappear!

I bought my second pair of runners the very next day in a Prada bow teek in Harajuku.

My feet were being carved into tiny hammers and I'd been too heel-struck to notice!

I've never looked back after my Hello Kitty agony in Tokyo. I still purchase the Hello Kitty bandaids but I'm also at a really, really remarkable stage in my life where my teenage son *refuses* to be seen with me *unless* I'm wearing 'cool runners' chosen for me, by *him*!

A mother can earn more points than a Frequent Flyer if she wears a pair of runners chosen for her by her son. My selection of 'Edward approved' runners are all purchased from the Savers superstore op shop in Brunswick. I know Ed loves me a *little bit* more when I'm wearing the coolest brand of runner in town, Asics (pronounced Az-icks). To be perfectly honest I don't *really* love the Asics. The featured 'mesh' component is rather weak and offers little protection if a brick falls on your foot.

And when Jack and I step in a puddle of dirty rainwater, Jack's paws and my feet are soaked. (I don't like red laces either but Ed just adores me in the Az-icks. He's so proud of me that once he took a photo of my Az-icks feet and put me on his Instagram story! He captioned it 'Steezy Pensioner', which I'm pretty sure means 'I have a really cool Mum!'

Postscript: A steezy pensioner is actually a homeless person who, by some minacious miracle, accidentally steps out in a pair of really cool runners. A podiatrist (yes, the same one!) told me that op-shop shoes are a breeding ground for ticks, shoe fleas and athlete's foot. I didn't know how to tell him I didn't have a running clue whose shoes I'd been wearing after he diagnosed me with two planter warts and *hammer toe*!

But before you abuse, criticise and accuse, I double dare you to walk a mile in a my sky-high shoes!

The apron strings of *lament*

For readers with children under twelve, I'm terribly sorry, but this chapter may alarm you. It might bring into question everything you've ever read about being a mother.

Two days ago, I vowed and declared I wouldn't cut apples or kiwi fruit into baby-sized mouthfuls ever again! I vowed to stop hand-feeding fruit into my son's hungry mouth and swore there'd be no more baby bottles filled with freshly brewed coffee. I promised myself I'd never hover in a dramatic fashion over his decorated cot with self-indulgent tears falling on his cute chubby cheeks. And as for his floral onesies, he could wash them himself!

My son had defied me, lied to me and broken the house rules too many times. He could find his own way to creche and all sleepovers were cancelled. I disconnected the internet so there would be no screen time.

Crafty!

I was on fire, making the consequences of his actions real, although I nearly caved when I saw his baby lips quivering and his eyes blinking with bitter disappointment.

'Too bad,' I said, sticking a dummy in his mouth. 'Too bloody bad! You shouldn't have defied me and lied to me! The Tokyo playdate is off, and you've only got yourself to blame!'

It only took two days to break my vows of punishment – a

new record for me. After Ed agreed to change his outlook on everything, he also agreed to try extra hard with everything else. He washed four plates, moved a saucer from the floor to the kitchen, and soaked a casserole dish in hot sudsy water (which I feel showed a real commitment to trying). He scribbled a note and said he'd peg the wet washing out on the line. Of course, I didn't believe him, but I'm a mother (forever) and so I *have* to.

You might be pleased to know that I've just delivered a Royal Doulton plate of bite-sized kiwi fruit with four slices of mango, topped off with a rose petal, into my son's bedroom, with a cup of freshly brewed coffee.

And the Tokyo play date? That's back on.

I was having trouble holding on, I was having trouble letting go, I was waiting on my baby man hand and foot, and breaking vows after I vowed and declared I wouldn't. I was always bitterly disappointed in myself when my resolve cracked, and even though he'd defied me, lied to me and broken the house rules, I was just like any other mum with a loving, ripped-to-shreds, resentful, hurtin' heart. I gave in.

You might be wondering how old my baby son is. He's eighteen (still just a baby!).

I'd tied my son to my apron strings with a triple-knotted bow of dependency, and a baby son tied with a triple knot is desperate to let go.

My baby child wants to travel to Japan and Nepal for two months, he wants to 'touch' the existential void and hunter-gather with a nomadic tribe in the Himalayan mountains. He wants to be reborn. To experience the mind-altering plant ayahuasca

(Ay-Oh-Was-Ka), and vomit his intestines and baby lungs up in a mountain cave in the Himalayas because that's what happens when you sip Ay-Oh-Was-Ka. You vomit your lungs up!

And do you know what the worst part is? He wants to experience life and travel to dangerous parts of the world alone.

Without me!

I don't believe vomiting up your insides in a mountain cave in the Himalayas is a good thing, and as for touching existential voids, he's got Buckley's!

And being reborn at eighteen without *me*? 'He's dreamin'!'

He wants to move out of our overly decorated pink apartment and into a shared house in Fitzroy. He hasn't thought through this fanciful adventure because who'd cut and dice his fruit and deliver freshly brewed coffee to his bedside? At midday? In an existential void? The tooth fairy? I don't think so!

Despite being forty years younger than me, he sleeps twice as long. I've seen stoats in the windows of taxidermists who showed more signs of life.

But, without my son's beating heart, his teenage bedroom would become just another room. I was terrified of this future empty room. I worried I'd sleep in his bed and look for washing on the floor. With Ed in a completely different house on the other side of the river, how was I expected to know where he'd been, who he was with, what time he got home, and what he'd had for dinner?

I realise this may well have been his point, but, like I said, I was having trouble backing off. I was having trouble holding on. I was having trouble letting go. *Nothing* about letting go comes naturally to me and, in fact, I don't entirely understand what 'letting go' actually means.

People with abandonment issues have a hard time processing the absurdity of 'letting go' because our expertise is holding on. Our children are meant to be the cure for love cancer, not the source of it. Love cancer eats away at your heart, creating waves of unrest, mistrust and a general all-over terrible feeling. I already knew that love cancer, without years of therapy and meditating with Buddhist monks on a thin grey blanket, could never be cured.

The irony was, I'd worked especially hard and very earnestly on raising an enigmatic, sharp, brilliant, provocative son with oodles of charisma. I taught him to avoid running with the pack or biting other children. I urged him to travel (big mistake) and if he couldn't be like me, to find someone like me to be with. I'd also encouraged him to think about ways to earn lots of money to keep me in the manner I deserved in my whiz-bang older age.

I had raised my son with my own unorthodox philosophy on how to be a caring, compassionate, supportive, comforting, selfless, altruistic, exemplary, grounded, liberated, giving, stickybeaking, wholehearted, whiz-bang, fair-dinkum world-class mum, giving him unwavering, unstoppable 24-carat-gold love. I was aglow with my inner mantra – 'Don't be like your parents, be the exact opposite.'

And I was! The *exact* opposite of my own mum and dad. I was a roaring Lion Queen, a warrior, a phone thrower, a soldier with overprotective killer instincts. I'd die in the blink of an eye for my child. I'd throw my body into a hot oven to keep him warm.

I'd go without, so he could have it all. He was in every breath I took, every stitch I sewed, forever glued to me like a thousand baby bows.

There wasn't a thing I wouldn't do to keep my son safe in this dangerous modern world, but after all I'd done for him, why would he choose to travel the world alone, without his mother?

One day he was in nappies loving me to death, and the next I was blindsided.

Sure, I'd felt the warning signs. I put them down to a contagious teenage virus and, like all splendid parents, I thought the mood swings were my fault.

His angry ball of weighted silence aimed at anything I said or did, and the point-blank refusal to do anything I asked, always followed by a boom and a bang as he vanished into his bedroom. I was desperate to snatch him back into my heart, but the sad, unholy truth is that teens are wired to untie the bow to our apron strings. They view us from a galaxy far, far away, and they target us as their most committed enemy. We take away their freedom, their civil and mental rights, we take away everything – we are mind control … and on top of all that, we play the undercover FBI parent game, interviewing their friends and teachers without any right to do so.

I didn't just *play* the undercover parent FBI parent game, I *was* the FBI game!

I went to great lengths to make sure I knew what my son was up to, without him knowing *a thing*. With masterful secret-service intelligence, along with my witchy gift for cracking passwords, I'd become a police informer. Four secret doof-doof techno parties and three house parties were shut down thanks to me. All of them dens of iniquity with alcohol and drugs!

So you can see the trouble I'm in and why I can't possibly allow my son to go to Nepal and Japan without me. Who would keep a spying eye on him? And the fruit? Who would cut it into bite-sized pieces?

And so I reached for Google's hand. Google said it's oh-so-normal for sons to become repelled by their mothers. Experts calmly say to ignore how our adored child's body spins into a tennis ball of resentment when we hover in their bedroom with a plate of cut-up fruit.

I wish I'd been warned about the phenomenal amount of hurt we endure when our kids pull away, leaving us gasping for air. The sinking loveless feeling as our child morphs into a mini adult feels like the slow and most painful breakup of all. Carl Jung writes that pulling away is completely normal. It means we've done a smashing job of growing our kids up and should be slapping ourselves on the back for creating such independent, fierce little creatures.

I wasn't slapping myself on the back for creating an independent, fierce little creature. My baby had stopped holding my hand and I was a social embarrassment whenever I reached.

I watch my son sleeping, and often appear 'bedside' in the hope I'll catch a glimpse of his baby face hidden inside the angsty one on the pillow. If I look really closely I can still see traces of the baby who turned into a man. I tried to photograph the baby face once, but he woke up mid-photograph. He still has nightmares about a hungry magpie with a huge bow on its beak taking iPhone snaps.

I feel redundant and unnecessary and frightened of who I might become without the boy who calls me Mum. I never got to properly say goodbye to all his changing faces and now he's almost a man. My eyes still light up whenever I see him and, while I know he loves me, I'm finding it impossible to grasp that his life no longer spins around me. Not anymore.

He leaves for Japan and Nepal in two weeks, and I don't know who or how I'll be without him. I might keep a record of our little lives, the laughs we had, the clothes we wore, and how I couldn't love a human soul more. I hope he doesn't touch any existential voids or find what he's looking for in Nepal. If he does, I'm in real trouble. Our children will always be the sun around which we spin, long after they've untied our apron strings. And their baby hands will be the only hands of which we can *never* let go …

Postscript: Speaking of suns, Japan and Nepal look *very* interesting at this time of year, and vomiting up my lungs on a beach in Nepal could be very beneficial for my spiritual growth. I've *always* wanted to look nomadic on a goat in the Himalayas. I just hope the hunter-gatherer tribes in Nepal know how to cut up fruit and serve freshly brewed coffee!

The parasol of *wanderlust*

D o you love a vacation? A holiday? A little jaunt away? Perhaps a staycation?

Of course you do! You're a normal, mood-swinging type of person. *Up* some days, *flat* on your holiday-less face the next. People who don't like a little jaunt away don't like change. They can be spartan, and prone to complaining and nitpicking. Some are a little joyless, obsessed with their work. I was one of those.

Some people prefer the staycation, where the whole family stays home and attends free events in the city. The kids might dig a hole, and you *might* clean the bath. You might even bake a cake and let the dog lick the spoon. A partner does very little to assist in organising activities for a staycation, which is always highly irritating.

I'm restless, subdued and panicked* whenever I need a jaunt away. I become exasperated, nervy, highly strung, and impulsively *snap* at the smallest of things. I cry over spilt milk and I've been known to hiss at dandelions.

When I was a full-time working girl I didn't care for holidays. I didn't take them and, worse still, I didn't believe in them. You don't take holidays when you're becoming successful – they're a

---

* Not many people can be subdued and panicked at the same time, but I can – it's a gift!

distraction. I changed the word to *helliday* just so I could say it out loud.

I thought holidays were for people who loved fine wine, smelly cheese and truffles from the Loire Valley, people who ate snails and bugs, and who loved the beach, the surf and the snow. Holidays were for people with close families.

I couldn't relate to any of that. I'd work for the rest of my life! And then I changed. After 1000 years of working full-time I'd had enough. I was going to Italy.

There were moments when I felt the tears from Italian clouds spilling all over me. I was soaked in helliday joy and, as much as I had baulked at the helliday, I began to understand what the cloud contained. Who knew a little jaunt away could bring respite?

A proper holiday changes your reality. You crave the entire holiday experience to feel alive and like you're not missing out on life, so that you're interesting, happening and on the move. You yearn to live in places you've never lived, and fantasise about a completely *different* reality.

One bright Byzantine afternoon, when I was roaming in Italy with my boyfriend, Hugo, I did something reckless and stepped into a completely different reality.

My yearning had really taken hold that day. I started mourning the fact I would *never* live off the fat of the land in a crumbling ruin in Tuscany, or buy five chooks from the local market, or have a barnyard of animals. I grew concerned that I'd *never* plant a vegetable garden or learn how to prepare gourmet treats. I fantasised about making the local villagers 'goth' fascinators and then opening a fascinating goth fascinator shop, with smoked truffles on the side.

Alannah's Fascinating Truffle Goth Teek, only in Italian.

I blame the paranormal holiday forces, those otherworldly voices, for my colossal, foolish and giddy mistake. This was the day I *accidentally* bought an apartment in the limestone capital of Sicily, Noto. You can't really blame me for feeling a connection with Noto. The fourth toe on my left foot had recently been entirely removed by a surgeon due to melanoma. I'd had a toe removed.

No toe.

Noto.

I thought it was a sign.

I was on the vacation of a lifetime, with my nine toes and a dead-duck fascinator superglued to my head. We'd spent the afternoon at a Sicilian beach, where I dog-paddled with a lace veil shielding my face from the burning Sicilian sun. I didn't stop with the veil! No! For full beach-body coverage I wore a floral frock, a cardigan and a cute pair of socks. I'd made little to no attempt to downgrade my 'after five' costumes and I refused to slip into a 'bather'. I hated the sun, the sand, the water and the beach light. A harsh Italian beach light shows up every little thing. It's why I dressed like a beekeeper for all beach activity. Day and night. People stared and laughed at my get-up but I didn't care. I was on helliday.

After the beach swim we went to an Italian restaurant, ate spaghetti and drank Negroni from tinted glasses. I was off my head with helliday joy and my Italian was *really* coming along. To humour Hugo (who spoke fluent Italian) I'd surprise him and the *entire* town with my recently acquired gems: 'Chow, bella … carbonara, marinara, amatriciana, parmigiana … margarita.'

I was drunk on the splendour of my own language skills.

We'd been playing the couples game on holiday of 'what if'. (I *know*. Smug comes to mind!) *What if* you had a studio in Noto? *What if* I became a poet? *What if* we retire in Noto? *What if* I live here and you live there? *What if* I just make you so tired with the 'what ifs' you fall dead asleep? *What if* I go out in the Noto magic hour and snoop through the back streets looking for answers to everything?

I had no idea I was about to buy a Byzantine apartment.

I was let loose to roam the limestone splendour as the magic hour drifted in. I needed to regroup. I crave solitude, and often need to regroup whenever I've been social for more than three hours. When I'm on a jaunt away, my regrouping can swing wildly. I was in a state of full wanderlust, staring in wonder at the architecture. My no-toe was stumbling around in the Noto heat, openly awed at the angelic cherubs with Italian signs hammered into their achingly beautiful faces.

Then I saw it: *In Vendita*.

I knew these words: For Sale.

I thought it was a sign!

(Stumbling on nine toes through town I'd noticed everything was In Vendita. Stores, villas, crumbling castles and even churches. *Why would anyone sell*, I asked myself? *Why?*)

Next to this sign, I stumbled across an Italian gentleman sweeping a sun-drenched, jasmine-packed balcony. He needed to sell! *Dio mio* (my god), I had hit the jackpot! Intuition told me he was a widower. Brooming perfect! His broom strokes were slow and pained, he was thin and stooped, and he kept his head down.

I could sense in his demeanour that he wanted to escape both this town *and* his apartment, so I took a risk and smiled up at him like a bella donna. He waved back, shouting, 'Ciao, bella!'

I shouted out in my best Italian, 'Chow! Carbonara! Amatriciana parmigiana!'

'Come in … come in, bella …'

Lo and behold, as easy as that, I was inside a private apartment in Noto, with an In Vendita sign nailed to a cherub's face outside.

The apartment was blindingly glorious. A long hallway with velvet-clad walls led me into a sunken lounge with emerald-green couches, and onto a countrified yellow kitchen I told myself was authentic and workable. I ignored the flashing fluorescent light flickering in the kitchen and convinced myself that it was the light from an original chandelier, fourteenth century. A black staircase wrapped itself around the flowery terrace and sinuous wrought-iron balconies glimmered in the Noto glow. The Italian widower swept me through doorways and into a lift that took me to two hidden attics. Could it *be* any more perfect?

He showed me the room at the end of the first passage, the room where his wife had died three months earlier. I planned to make this into a rollicking Italian guestroom after I ridded the place of the ghost.

'Graaaappa?' he asked.

Grappa? I'd never tried grape juice. The widower gave me a wine glass full of it and I drank the whole lot. I had an instant need to vomit. It wasn't grape juice, it was 60 per cent alcohol.

He poured me another grappa in a curved glass and I somehow drank that too. I was high on the holiday juices. High on life. High on Byzantine architecture, high on grappa, but in the distance a chorus of holiday voices were daring me, whispering, *Your own apartment in Noto … going … going …*

I didn't want to miss out.

Had I not moved on from my glory days? My alternative to a helliday in my roaring twenties was to take a drive around Kew, Canterbury and Ivanhoe looking for auctions on a Saturday afternoon. I favoured massive family homes, six to seven bedrooms, preferably with converted stables, a pool/spa type of situation and a rose garden the size of a small suburb. And a shed. Maybe even a vegetable patch with electric fencing.

I'd zoom through the family home, high-heeled, craving and *raving*, not yet aware of the joy in a proper holiday and looking for an alternative reality. I'd try to laugh prettily with the other buyers taking in all of the house's history on my four-hour helliday.

I'd note how the plates were stacked in the family-sized kitchen and if the china was Doulton or Royal Albert, and what kind of food the vendor favoured in the family fridge. I'd move onto the wife's wardrobe to see if she wore nice clothes. One time I accidentally broke a bottle of Chanel No 5, and another time I dipped myself in the pool (fully clothed) just before the auction. It was 45 degrees Celsius!

These were the days when, dazed, I convinced myself that not only was I *raising* prices through the roof in Kew, Canterbury and Ivanhoe, but I was also upping the price of the family home I'd just barged in on. I thought I was a born realtor. I spoke with sound knowledge and a know-all lilt to my voice about real-estate valuations and fake vendor bids. I'd charm the auctioneer, spinning untruths about how I *could* be the new owner, waving a cheque book for dramatic effect.

Before the auction I'd sneak a biscuit and stand to the left of the real prospective buyers. In view but still mysterious, I hoped I looked like a prospective buyer, waving my cheque book around so everybody could see. When the auctioneer's booming voice began, the biscuit would crumble in my hot little hand.

'We are ON the MARKET ... this glorious blue-chip family home WILL be sold today ... Are we all done at four-and-a-half? Are we all out? Ladies and gentlemen, please wait here while I refer to *the vendor* ...'

This was when the real fun started. I couldn't contain myself. 'This bewdiful family home has now been confirmed ... WE ARE ON THE MARKET ... WE ARE GOING UP IN TENS ... we may go up in twenties ... maybe thirties ... awwwwww let's go the big FIFTY! Are we selling at four-and-a-half ... we are going up in tens, ladies and gentlemen ... We are on the market and going up in TENS!'

My crumbling biscuit would involuntarily fly over my head and before I knew it, I was going up in tens.

'We have a BUYER ... And wow, it's a FEMALE buyer ... gotta big family moving in, have ya, love? WE ARE GOING UP in tens ... that's four-and-a-half with a ten ... what about another ten ... GOING, GOING ...'

At this stage of the helliday auction, I'd crumble like a biscuit. I'd bid against myself. My hands would go up and down like a yo-yo. I peed my pants at an auction once and at another my nose started bleeding, blood spurting everywhere. I think it was because I was the last bidder on a family home with a teenage retreat and a spa. (I got out of that conundrum when a late bidder, thank *God*, arrived on the scene.)

I knew my flailings at auctions were part of my search for home. I was always looking for a reboot, a new reality. I'd made the same mistake before, yet here I was about to make it again! I didn't know where home was. I hadn't found it yet … but filled with the romance of the holiday, I had a *very strong* feeling it was in a Byzantine Rococo town in Italy.

Drawn into the future with sweet grappa on my lips, I told myself I'd matured. That I wasn't recklessly and impulsively purchasing another real-estate mistake in an attempt to find home. *What if* this was home?

I drank another grappa and ate Italian chocolate with Giuseppe and recklessly sallied forth, handing him a deposit. Two thousand euro! *Cash!* Giuseppe stashed it inside a glass jar and led me to a card table with two chairs on either side. On the table was paper with an official letterhead and a single bright-red pen. Giuseppe sat me on one of the chairs and pointed at the purchase price, dates, times, signatures … deposit, lawyers' fees … all in Italian, so I *think* that was what they were. It wasn't feeling very holidayish but I played along.

'I might have another grappa, I've never tasted anything so damn fine … yeah, yeah, yeah … I love it … show me around one more time … What did your wife die of, love? You must miss her terribly, and did she die right there, in *that* spot, right next to the jar of Polish pickles?'

He nodded solemnly.

I nodded solemnly back.

He didn't speak a word of English, but we got on famously.

In my mind, I'd already transported my clothing and antique furniture onto waiting ships, and remodelled the room where his wife had died into a stylish Italian dressing room.

I signed the document with the bright-red pen and Giuseppe beamed. I think I probably screamed!

I hurried back through the limestone streets to dazzle Hugo with my impetuous Noto purchase. 'I just bought an *apartment,* love. It's got two attics and jasmine growing wildly! Attics! What if we just moved here and lived off the fat of the land in Noto?'

What if?

I pulled out the paper I'd signed and slammed it on the grand piano like a dame in *The Art of the Deal.* 'Howzat!'

Howzwhat!

Hugo wasn't as delighted as me. He thought I'd been ripped off by the Mafia.

The next morning, and the one after that, and the *next* one after that and the next one after that, Hugo tried to nuke the deal. He told me that Giuseppe had disappeared with my wad of cash and the keys to my new apartment. Giuseppe wasn't answering his phone, and so we visited him in the flesh. We stood outside my new front door, my parasol of wanderlust catching the gentle grey morning rain. Giuseppe didn't look as widower-ish in the morning light. He looked like a mob boss who'd just murdered his wife! He told Hugo he was on his way out. Giuseppe and I glared fruitlessly at each other. The flowery jasmine hung limply, and the sun-drenched balcony was *dark.* The entire street needed a good sweep.

Noto broke my heart with its timeless wonder and promise of a brand new world ... but I had to face reality, and I hadn't thought the whole thing through. (A sub-problem of the holiday – you don't think things through.)

We crave a holiday not to escape life, but for life *not* to escape us. A true holiday is the moment when you dream of really living abroad in an apartment in Italy, being on permanent holiday ... you dream of change that comes from within: eternal and persistent. My wanderlust was yet another sign I was looking for other realities, in houses that would never feel like home.

Looking back to my working days, I was naive to ban myself from holidays, doing everything I could to become successful. I was naive to think it would be that easy. But as a newcomer to the holiday experience I was also naive to think I could have the holiday feeling *forever*. All year round.

Postscript: Hugo and I stayed five extra days while he artfully got me out of the deal and got all my euro back. I'm not banned from Noto or anything nasty like that – apparently, it's just better if I never return.

The hand mirror of *shame*

When was the last time you glanced into your hand mirror and spoke to your guilty little reflection?

'*Shame* on you, girl! Shame on *you* for saying and thinking that! You should be ashamed of yourself!'

I credit myself with *thinking* I know a colossal amount about shame and how we use shame tactics to survive our shameless little lives.

Shame is my *thing*. And if you're not yet attuned to the fact that my childhood growing up in Tasmania was jam-packed with shame and misery, well, without going *on* and on and *on* for hours and hours and hours, I'm the know-all of shame!

Toxic shame, disappointment shame, unrequited-love shame, childhood shame, jealousy shame – I know-all of *all* the shames!

Alannah, the shame know-all.

I even have a cousin named Shame. His real name is *Shane* but I thought it was Shame. Shame Hill. We didn't see Shame Hill a lot when I was growing up, and I presumed it was because he was living with so much shame, especially with a name like Shame.

Shame whispers to us of our limits and boundaries (if we've got any), but if we can catch our shame before it pulls us down the slippery slope of self-denigration we can stumble upon something very important about ourselves. Shame influences so many of our defences, character traits, reactions and non-reactions that I respectively award shame the winner of negative feelings! Hands down!

Shame is defined as the feeling of a deep, innate flaw, a feeling that makes you think that you are unworthy of companionship, compassion and love. We all experience shame, but some of us are able to douse it with an illicit flammable gas. I call these people the 'sham shifters' as they have crafty techniques that allow them to drop the 'e' from shame and turn it into a *sham*. The shame game has been going on from the day we were born, but if you were brought up in a safe, loving loungeroom with a turntable and parents who took a genuine interest in your life, you tend to soar above your shame.

We all feel the burn from childhood, from triggered memories when you were told that listening to music and dancing was a heathen act ... and if you were caught enjoying it, *Shame on you, girl!*

Shame is the swampland of the soul, a hangover from being teased when you were young, or from being too fat, or too thin, or not cool enough, or from always being the last one chosen for everything. We're all paddling underneath, in an effort to hide our shame.

In the way I love a scarlet woman, I also love a shamed woman (and I don't mean that in quite the way it sounds). I intuitively designed clothing for shamed scarlet women. I used to love dressing up the broken, shamed customers who absent-mindedly walked into one of my Alannah Hill bow teeks. I learnt to spot them long before they spotted me.

One of the things I miss about my glory days at Alannah Hill is the opportunity to demonstrate the power of dressing up. Woman have the gift of being able to forget their shamed little selves when they feel like a million dollars ... especially when they've only spent $999!

For me, dressing up women wasn't about making money, it was about how a shamed woman dressed up (to look *like meeee!*) would come alive in her ruffles, silk and feathers. And how the new Alannahfied woman waved goodbye from the bow-teek door, her shame gleefully left behind, scattered all over the floor.

So now, I'm here to help you understand that everything we know about shame is a little bit of a sham.

Guilt is often closely linked to shame but it's an entirely different thing. Guilt can be a positive emotion when you can admit to your shortcomings, but good old shame is what crucifies you for not being perfect. Guilt is a feeling of unsteadiness and discomfort, an emotional tool that informs your moral compass, values and opinions, while deep-rooted shame, if it's left unattended, will eat away at your wellness, forcing you to make time for your illness.

Without a loving loungeroom, I've learnt that there are only two ways to deal with shame – you either pretend it doesn't exist (which doesn't actually work and often leads to jail and a grim, angry life) or you learn how to become more resilient to shame and start to care less. No one really cares about our shame, we eventually learn, but there's a wise old saying, 'You can't put a wise head on young shoulders.'

When I had young shoulders, listening to music was a Hill family crime. We didn't have a record player, and if we showed any interest in music, it was not only a crime, it was a *mortal sin*. If you were caught trying to listen to music you were immediately classed as a lazy mongrel who needed to be watched. A mongrel looking for pleasure. My parents didn't believe in children basking in childhood pleasures, because we might have some fun. They had no time for fun, and if it looked like we were having any, it was shot down with flaming shame.

If you were caught watching *Countdown*, the whole family joined in for the shame game. I was once caught moving my head upon hearing the *Waltons* theme music. I was shamed for seeking pleasure and told I had a dumb American mind and to turn the fucking idiot box off. Only with hindsight can I now understand that being shamed for having 'a dumb American mind' had nothing to do with me. I could even be a little ashamed for thinking it did! But I remember the feeling of crushing shame. That kind of shame leaves a stain that's hard to wipe away.

Of course, shame comes in many shames and sizes, all tweaked to a fundamental fragility in our psyche. I was deeply offended by my parents' disapproval of my yearning for the tune, and I couldn't understand their harsh judgements.

It's taken me this long to come to terms with it.

I've only recently discovered the Rolling Stones are from England and not from LA. I know the Beatles are from London and the Flaming Lips' lead singer is someone called Wayne. My son knows more about music than I do, and because I'm a superb mother I allow him to listen to any music he wants *with no shame*.

Of course, my shame problem isn't really about music, it's about being caught listening to it on my own. Unfortunately *that* little shame my parents instilled in me has stayed *long* after it should have been gone.

If I wanted to hear music when I was a girl, I'd hide in the back seat of my father's car. I'd cover myself in a jumper and turn the dial straight to the golden oldies station. Unfortunately, one Sunday afternoon, mid 'Take It to the Limit' by the Eagles, I was discovered. My father went mental and the car keys were confiscated. I'd run the car battery down four times that month with my crime of listening to golden oldies and, like most petty crims, it wasn't long before I crimmed again. The lack of golden oldies and my intense need to listen to music resulted in what my mum called a 'breaking and interfering with'.

One afternoon after school I broke and entered into my eldest brother's community house that he was sharing with a mate called Cracker Jack. Cracker Jack had an LP collection and a record player with hifi speakers nailed to a wall. I'd heard Fleetwood Mac's 'Second Hand News' on the golden oldies station and, like a 'Farmer's Daughter', I needed to hear more.

I *entered* the community house through my brother's open window like a musically deprived Gold Dust Woman who couldn't Go Her Own Way like a Songbird, to get my fill of Fleetwood Mac.

When my brother arrived home he got a real shock to find me dancing like a gypsy to 'Second Hand News' with one of his VBs in my hand. I'd never felt freer until my brother turned up. I took on the shame of being kicked out but, really, was he the one who should have felt ashamed? I'd done him a few favours in the past, like the time I found a giant-sized bag of what looked like grass under the couch. I knew it was untoward and illegal, and I left the bag of green under his pillow with a note saying, 'I found this and I think it's yours.'

I saved him from the wrath of my father, and the very least he could do was allow me to listen to Fleetwood Mac. The flat's window was open anyway so *technically* I didn't break in, I only entered.

Until I was twenty-five years old I'd never owned a record, an LP, a cassette, a radio or a boom box.

In my eighties nightclub heyday, I was the first on the dance floor with choreographed dance routines that I picked up from watching *Young Talent Time*. My nan was obsessed with *YTT* and she let me watch it whenever I stayed with her. It was incredible, watching singing and dancing without any shame!

It was my nan who gave me the confidence to believe that I had the talent to become an actual *YTT* member. She gave me eight out of ten after witnessing my uncanny ability to grind, tap and perform a Highland Fling all at the same time.

It was also my nan who pointed out the glaring problem. My hair. It was thin and straggly with no natural ability to 'shine'. In two shakes of a head, any hopes of being part of the *YTT* family were dashed. Nan said that no matter how well I danced, unshiny, stringy hair on an apple-sized head like mine meant that *YTT* wouldn't want me, and I've been ashamed ever since! (I bought a shiny black wig from an op shop, so *technically* speaking my hair did shine!)

I've often wondered what my nan would feel if she saw me smashing it up on dance floors. A kick here, a tap dance in the middle of a robot dance followed by a belly dance and a mixture of the Highland Fling and freeform jazz ballet. I was always in control, never drunk or disorderly, which helped my moves on the dance floor. People *thought* I was letting go because of my wild dance moves. I was just showing off and trying to get maximum attention to cover my flaming shame.

Before I learnt to drive, my boyfriend Steven would often find me propped up in the seat of his Wolseley listening to the golden oldies station in the garage with the car heater on. He replaced the car battery eight times before he finally left the Wolseley spluttering on the side of the road, the frail girl from the Carpenters harmonising in the background …

It was only when I bought a white 1970s Peugeot with a built-in radio/cassette player that I really started to let go of my music shame. The cassette player lit itself up when I turned it on. In my own space, with nobody judging my stunted childhood music taste, I found a place to call my own and listen to music with no shame.

I used to go missing for days in that white Peugeot.

A car is really just another room to call your own, a private space where you can listen to music and not feel shamed. I still have most of my grandest creative ideas in the car. For me, a car with music is a kind of pure freedom. A place where I'm free to fantasise and change my mood, a place where I find solutions to a vast array of various unsolvable problems. Madonna, Lana Del Rey, Fleetwood Mac and Patsy Cline can lift my mood sky high, or if I want to feel sad and way down low, there's always Cowboy Junkies and the Best of the Seekers. If I want to plan a fashion party, I turn to the Rolling Stones, Sonic Youth and the Vienna Boys' Choir.

I can't wipe away the shaming I endured as a girl, and it would be wrong to say I did. I didn't overcome the shame, but I learnt to 'find a way around it', despite not having shiny hair. I'll always be a little bit jealous when I see people lost in music, their eyes closed with a strange look of ecstasy. And I'll always be giddily amazed at their blithe disregard at being seen on planes, bikes or even in the streets, their ears in a pair of Bose headphones, enthralled in silent music ecstasy. I've always been too ashamed to don a pair of Bose – people would know I was enjoying music *publicly*. But I've worked out how to make the closing of the eyes work for me. It's a great way to avoid people talking drunkenly to you. Close your eyes and *pretend* you're lost in music and people can't talk to you! There's a lot of freedom in that.

Every single one of us is affected in dubious, haunting and shimmering ways with our reactions to and feelings about shame. We don't understand what it means to live through a traumatic and loveless childhood until it's well over. To unpick the shame thrashing around from my childhood I knew I required a 'shame exorcism'.

Shame holds back our reinvention for years. When we hold shameful secrets, they become a great barrier to success and an even greater barrier to living a peaceful, happy life. As we grow older, we care less about the colossal number of issues that dwarfed us when we were younger; things that once made us squirm with shame. We cared deeply about anything and everything but, mostly, what other people thought of us.

And being excluded

And being laughed at

And being ridiculed

And missing out

And being made to feel ashamed.

To be honest, loves, there *is* a way of healing even our most painful, shameful experiences. As with most poisons, the toxicity of shame needs to be neutralised by something else. It starts with a C and ends with an N.

If you're thinking 'curtain', *shame* on you! It's *compassion*.

Compassion is the one true antidote to shame.

What we need to remember when we're running wild with shame is that we also carry the capacity to feel *unlimited* compassion. Compassion for our shamed past selves, for our present selves, and for the other shamed people paddling hard alongside us.

When you next look into the hand mirror of shame, just remember, loves, that shame is nothing but a great big sham!

The faux
fur of
the fume

Are you weary of feeling outbursts of anger? Sick to death of fuming? Annoyed and *outraged* by the smallest of things?

I am. I've been angry, fuming, annoyed and *outraged* for two decades. Anger in a woman is a sign she's been deeply hurt by the world and everybody around her, the hurt bottling itself up as *rage*.

No matter our age, dear reader, women are really, really angry because there's a lot to be angry about! Get ready to be forty because that's when our real anger comes out! A premenopausal woman brings a lot of wisdom, grace and poise to life. She doesn't suffer fools, and often enjoys a wine (or six) of an evening to block out her burning rage. Unfortunately, a woman over forty also carries a suitcase of jagged emotion that psychologists liken to anger. I call it 'The Fume'.

Now, dear reader, The Fume can happen to the best of us, anytime, anyplace, anywhere. In fact it's probably happening to you right now.

The Fume can simmer on low heat for days, like a witch's cauldron loaded with poisonous berries and lemon rind … simmer simmer simmer *fume fume* simmer simmer *fume fume* simmer. Simmering eventually boils right over like milk left on a hot plate, staining the stovetop with a residue of burnt cream.

As I grew older, my outbursts of fury were becoming more frequent, and people were starting to notice. I started to take out my rage on other people. One particular fume-fuelled week, I pulled a driver over with my howling new police siren (purchased on eBay for $129, with three volumes – naturally I used the loudest). It's quite remarkable what people do when they hear a police siren … they *all* pull over!

In the same week I threatened a truck driver with a phony $250 fine for abusive behaviour and, not long after, I sideswiped another driver's car after he roared at me for changing lanes without using an indicator.

When people asked, 'How are you?' I'd reply, 'Fuming. I'm bloody *fuming*!'

When people texted me and asked, 'How are you?' I'd reply, '*Fuming*. I'm *bloody* fuming!'

People thought I was joking … but I wasn't. I'd fume if my favourite checkout girl at the IGA wasn't friendly enough on the register, I'd fume at Ed's teachers if they suggested I wasn't teaching Ed the value of homework, I'd fume at stray cats, at my hair that wouldn't tease, at indolent teenagers, know-it-all teenagers, loved-up couples , dog owners, neighbours, the iPhone charger that kept going missing, Telstra's call-back line, the ATO, crowds, malls, most people … I could write a list of 10,000 things and still I wouldn't be done.

I was shoutier and hissier than an alley cat without an alley, and I feared if something didn't change soon, that pissed-off alley cat would be me.

I thought getting rich quick might cure The Fume.

How rich are you? How rich am I?

Not rich enough, I hear you cry.

Yes, I was under the greatest delusion of all time – that if I became filthy, filthy rich, I'd stop fuming at the smallest of things. I thought being filthy rich would enable me to live a more spontaneously en*rich*ing life in which I'd be happier and kinder. We're all guilty of wishfully thinking that being filthy, filthy rich will cure our problems.

I controlled my fuming with fantasies.

Masquerading as both Bonnie *and* Clyde, I planned to rob a bank in a small suburb on the outskirts of Melbourne. I'd already cased the joint and given a fair amount of thought to a black getaway car and the kind of bag I should take to fill with $100 notes.

In other moments of greediness, I would turn to Tom Ford for inspiration. As one of the world's most famous fashion designers, Tom is super rich and super cool, and I owned several pairs of his sunglasses. Wearing a faux-fur mink coat and a pair of jet-black Tom Fords on my inquisitive face, I'd imagine asking Tom, 'How can I become independently wealthy, prosperous and unbearably, horribly well off? Tom, how can I get filthy, *filthy* rich?'

(Tom never answered. He was too rich.)

My fantasies began to escalate. I imagined purchasing a powder-blue Rolls-Royce from Jackie Collins's podiatrist – fancy gold lettering on the front numberplate spelling 'FILTHY', even fancier silver lettering on the back numberplate spelling 'RICH'.

Dripping in wealth, I'd welcome Joan Rivers along for the ride. In my fantasy, Joan was immortal, and she'd spot my powder-blue Rolls-Royce in valet parking at Saks Beverly Hills. Joan would be thrilled by the likes of me, filthy rich and all dressed up like Zsa Zsa Gabor, hurtling across the intersection of Hollywood and Vine in my powder-blue Rolls. As I ran from the car in sky-high Prada heels, Joan and her bejewelled microphone would be suddenly thrust at my plumped-up filthy-rich lips ...

'Alaaaaarnaaaaah! How did you get *so* filthy rich?'

(That would be the name of Joan's new hit HBO show – *How'd You Get So Filthy Rich?*)

'With an *idea*, Joan. I made nothing into something with something that did nothing.'

I can hear you wondering how someone like me, drowning in bottomless seas of depth, intensity and intelligence, could ponder such vapid notions of wealth. 'What's WRONG with you, Alannah? Being rich doesn't make people happy! Look at Britney Spears, Madonna, Jackie Onassis, Justin Bieber and Barbara Woolworth Hutton.* Alannah, you're even *worse* than I thought!'

No. I was *not* worse than you thought.

I was *much* worse!

Some nights I itched and scratched like Itchy and Scratchy, itching for a cure and scratching when I couldn't find it. I lay awake for weeks, dreaming I lived inside an ATM.

---

* Ms Woolworth Hutton inherited the modern equivalent of more than a billion dollars when she was twenty-one years old. In desperate need of love, she married seven times, but men didn't make her happy, making her life one endless tragedy and heartache after the next. Barbara Hutton died alone, bankrupt and addicted to pills and alcohol in her suite at the Beverly Wiltshire Hotel in 1979. She was sixty-six. She was the real 'poor little rich girl'.

Alannah's
Trillion
Millions

Of course I didn't actually want to live inside a miserable, desolate ATM, but I did want to be surrounded by a stash of money. And so the real question remained: how was I going to get filthy rich?

It took me a while to find the answer but, as with all filthy little questions, a suitcase full of bitcoin soon hit me on the side of the head. Bingo! *The internet*!

I don't care for Facebook's gormless, robotic, unlikable founder, but Facebook *did* make him a trillionaire. I couldn't do anything that involved *social networking* even if it was only online – computer mistakes fanned my flaming fume! I wouldn't get rich that way. But Facebook owned apps … and they'd been downloaded sixteen billion times! I worked out that if I took, say, even a *tenth* of Zucker-bug's market, I *could* be filthy, *filthy* rich in less than a year. There was the answer, that was it!

I needed to create an app.

Instagram influencers had their own apps. I wasn't an Instagram influencer, but I had an eye for detail, and a knack for knowing what women wanted. They wanted stress-free lives, with no mistakes and a cure for their rage. A cure for The Fume.

My computer knowledge was extraordinarily limited, and I had no interest in understanding how to actually *make* a rage-curing app. I'd failed to grasp what a URL was, and I thought a server was somebody who served me with court documents. And as far as 'the cloud' was concerned, all I knew was that I would like to fly there.

Once, I accidentally downloaded over 1000 personal photos onto all my social media accounts – images of me dressed up like a housewife wearing sexy lingerie, a cat wrapped around my neck, and a black thigh-high leather high-heeled boot. (The type of tawdry images *nobody* is meant to view because the images are meant to be *hidden* in the cloud!) I was convinced I'd been hacked, but a Genius Bar nerd told me I'd hacked myself.

So I knew there was no way I could design an app, despite having a keen, arty app eye. Instead, I did the sensible thing and paid a professional. The app-building office sat crookedly above a fish and chip shop in Smith Street, Fitzroy. And it was in the crooked app building, amid the stench of fish-and-chip oil and rancid batter, that Simon and I created my incredible app. I called it The Fume.

The prototype was phenomenal. It appeared on your screen as a gently pulsating, blood-red heart. For a measly fifty cents a download, the app promised a cure for rage.

Imagine the money that would flow my way! I was dreaming in $100 notes.

Press on the heart and a mesmerising pearlescent light shone, a distant angel sang, bluebirds flew across the screen and images of a Von Trapp child dressed in curtains winked and sang 'Do-Re-Mi'. You could stare at it for hours, iridescent nothingness drawing you gently into a meditative state. The app would help women (and men) dissociate from their fury while making me filthy, filthy rich!

The beauty of it was that there were no ads, no interruptions, no password to remember. Just looking into the nothingness would make all fury disappear. The power of seeing something in nothing would immediately soothe and smooth our jagged, fuming edges. And despite my app having no *real* function, just staring into nothingness was a pathway to digitise meditation in a world where people are superglued to their phones.

Brilliant!

At fifty cents a download, the app was a steal.

I'd be filthy rich in a week.

I couldn't sleep, dance, eat or walk in a straight line a week before launch date. I moved at light speed. It's a well-known fact that when moments away from becoming a billionaire, one doesn't just move fast, one *zooms* past! I was a whisper shy of my lifelong dream ... no more sorrow, no more stress.

Four sleeps before launch date, I was basking on a daybed dressed up as Rita Hayworth and pretending to drink martinis. In less than a week, I'd be filthy rich and rage-free. Like a caged chicken ready to be set free, I could see the powder-blue Rolls rolling toward me in the distance.

My phone beeped: it was the genius nerdy code developer. I purred down the phone like a sycophantic alley cat.

'Hello, Simon, what's up?' *Purr, purr.*

'Alannah, BIG problem. You know the forty-five people we tested the app on?'

'Yes, The Fume! It's a miracle machine!'

'Aaaah, in a way, but ... how can I put it? We're getting complaints.'

'Who from? Jeff Bezos? He's just jealous!'

'Alannah, it's a mess. Most people are refusing to go back to work and some look like they've been programmed for a cult. Grown men are watching infomercials and crying over WorkCover ads. Some are playing Monopoly. And some are fat and don't even care anymore! They're *hypnotised* by The Fume. So ahhhh ... yeah ... The Fume app mostly seems to cure fuming, but once the fuming's gone, you've got forty-five wannabe Dalai Lamas and the world can't survive with just lamas.'

I was confused. Dismayed. One hundred per cent convinced The Fume would be a fuming hit, I'd been far too busy preening as Rita Hayworth to test the app myself. I looked at my phone with the tech magician's voice droning on in the background. I stared at the pulsating red heart ... the angels flew and the music calmed me almost immediately.

Calmed me so much that the horror came surging up.

Had I accidentally invented an antidepressant app? Is that all it would take, a fifty-cent app to cure global depression and rage?

With a cold, shrinking sensation I felt my fire going out ... my vision blurring beige, my desire withering, my blood turning cold. Every sequin in the world dulled as one.

I asked myself, what would the world be like if everybody was de-fumed? Joyless, passionless, neutered ... a neutral, bland world I would never want to live in.

I was in gentle revolt with myself for having nearly brought this app into reality. 'Kill it!' I yelled *uncalmly* at the tech guru. 'Kill The Fume now! I can't be held responsible for such an aberration!'

And just like that, I turned my back on one 100 billion dollars. I'm fuming just thinking about it!

Deep down, I know a real cure for The Fume cannot be found on the internet. The internet is where half The Fume comes from: a place where rage breeds and festers. A cure for fury cannot be bought, sold or rented, and to be really honest ... I'm not sure I want my fume to be totally *fumigated*.

The real question is how we *contain* The Fume without it consuming us and sending us mad. We need The Fume like a spinster needs a romantic fling, like a guitar needs a string. We need our dreams and relentless awareness, and without The Fume we have no claws with which to fight for our dreams ...

We're all born screaming and our screams never stop!

Postscript: On itchy and scratchy nights, I still dream about becoming filthy, filthy rich. Admit it, you do too. You're probably thinking about it right now! The filthy part of the whole damned thing is that even though we know being filthy, filthy rich isn't a cure, the itch to be rich never really stops. (Until we die ... and because I'm ageless I can't die.) And so, my loves, I fume on ...

The cardigan of *solitude*

If I spy an unclean sock on my bedroom floor it makes me want to disappear.

It doesn't matter whether I adore the unclean-sock owner, the sight of that sock makes me want to wail. But instead, I disappear.

The sight of a man's well-worn honking sock will eventually make *all* women want to disappear. We've smelt enough honking socks and smelly feet to last a lifetime.

Science has proven that women have seven million *extra* smelling neurons than men, and it's all to do with a thing in our brains called the 'olfactory bulb'. That bulb is the number one reason why men can't smell truly awful odours, especially their own – they don't have enough neurons. But women *excel* in the smelling fields. We're practically beagles. Our eggs begin to die off from the moment we're born, so God gave us a special gift – the gift of a highly tuned sense of smell. Men can't smell their own honking feet and it's why they claim innocence when asked, 'Did something die or is that just … your honking feet?'

They're *genuinely* unable to whiff their own honking smells, and with only half the smelling neurons women have, how could they? Which leads me to four questions:

Why tolerate it?

Why wash the socks?

Why live with the owner of the offending sock?

Why not live life as a LAT?

Curious as to what a LAT is? It's people who are Living Apart Together. They *choose* to live apart. Living Apart Together gives people all the advantages of autonomy, plus all the pleasures of intimacy. It's the opposite to being a CUD (Cohabitating Under Duress).

You don't mess with people who have a LAT kind of philosophy.

Gwyneth Paltrow and her husband, Brad Falchuk, are a super example of what the media call 'high-functioning LATs'. Brad and Gwyneth show the world how you can run a multi million–dollar online business selling candles that smell just like Gwyneth's vagina! Gwyneth and Brad are in 'in love' but they choose to live in separate houses. And I know what you're thinking: they live apart because of Gwynny's smelly candle, but you'd be incorrect! Gwynny says they live apart because she doesn't want to see Brad seven nights a week!

Victoria and David Beckham are also classed as LATs because their mansion is so expansive that it spreads across two suburbs. Posh lives in the east wing with her postcode and David lives in the west wing with another. Posh!

LAT men can only be with LAT women. It's very important to repeat that sentence: LAT men can only be with LAT women.

I cannot stress the importance of repeating it again: *LAT men can only be with LAT women.*

LATs are independent, romantic and headstrong. They crave solitude, trust less, overthink and shut most people out! They place a great deal of value on their relationship, and trust is their biggest asset. Once trust has gone, it causes a catastrophic breakdown with grave results: usually a breakup.

I've been a LAT for almost twenty years and, once you've lived this way, there is no going back. I have only lived with two men, and the last one was my son's dad, Karl. I told myself I'd never live with a man again, and I haven't. Nobody wants to see their partner seven nights a week, but people forget all about that when they live together.

I live with my teenage son, Ed, and I'm doing everything I can to keep him tied to my apron strings. I've discovered that you can still enjoy the LAT lifestyle with a teen because once you're accustomed to their chill, and grasp the spine-tingling fact that we love and need our children *more* than they love and need us, living with a teen is *almost* bearable!

I'm also aware too much solitude can turn into loneliness – this is where living with a teenager can be very advantageous. But still, I'd rather be lonely than slowly going mental from CUD. Wouldn't you?

We all need a room to call our own when our hearts go quiet and the birds stop singing. The natural creativity in all of us, the sudden and slow insights, the bursts of ideas and gentle bubbles of imagination are all the result of being alone. I need solitude to figure things out, to unearth new discoveries and find new answers to everything I asked about yesterday. Solitude allows my unconscious to process and to unravel the thousands of problems I carry about unnecessarily. Without solitude, I'd struggle to have an original idea and, to be honest, our best ideas are thought up when we're totally alone.

I worry about people who can't be alone.

When I lived with Karl, I didn't understand a man's quiet heart or how solitude worked. I took everything personally. When he finally left, I was determined not to make the same mistake ever again! I swore I'd be a LAT *forever*.

Even now, I put a lot of pressure on myself to look taller, thinner, younger and relevant. A lot of men fail to understand how many hours go into suddenly appearing as an ageless, highly strung, kabuki porcelain doll. I don't want my partner to know that transforming from a little beige nobody into a sugar-coated somebody takes three hours!

My secrets are kept under close guard. The secret to looking like a double for Marilyn Monroe comes about with hours and hours of alone time and the strategic placement of hundreds of tea lights to convince people I have a Venus body, a little like Marilyn's.

But candlelight and body scrub are not all you need; it's not as easy as that! You need to be able to be alone. Learning how to be alone can take years, and the only way to practise is by *being* alone!

I wouldn't want a living soul knowing I put Johnson's baby powder in my hair (to reduce oil build-up) or that it takes two hours to puff up my hair into a bouffant tiger's roaring mane. I'd have a meltdown if anyone discovered I used the haemorrhoid creams Anusol and Rectinol to reduce fine lines and puffiness around my eyes. Imagine if anybody found those twin tubes? Nobody would ever believe it was for freezing fine lines around the eye area!

One evening years ago Hugo discovered I was a full-time functioning LAT. His ears pricked right up as I sipped a Diet Coke and explained that the world was full of independent, creative women living an alternative lifestyle as LATs. He seemed genuinely overjoyed with the whole LAT movement, and warmed to it immediately.

It's taken me a decade to understand the difference between a dark, smouldering mood and a quiet, contemplative one. I don't react very well to a 'smouldering mood' but bohemian musician types revel in them. They live like fruit bats, upside down and smouldering in darkness. I've learnt that it's best for me if they 'smoulder' in their own dark space.

Listen up and on high volume, loves: take it from me, there is zero point in trying to change a LAT, especially those over thirty-five. Most people only change when they're faced with their own mortality, or when a crisis of great magnitude presents itself.

One of the key things about being a LAT is giving your partner space for their private things in your private space. I gave Hugo a drawer in a gorgeous Florentine mirrored bureau, and he was quick to learn that his shoes and socks, once removed, were not permitted to be seen. We have a much better evening when they're nowhere to be found. But it's important to set the ground rules too. Draping clothing on furniture is frowned upon in the apartment, and snorting in the shower gives me nightmares.

LATs naturally gravitate toward comfort, and my airy Art Deco apartment is *very* comfortable (perhaps a little *too* comfortable!). I've decorated, styled and over-stuffed it with embellished satin cushions and velvet Marie Antoinette–style couches. To make it more inviting, everything is in various shades of pink. I sleep in a king-sized mirrored bed while my lovely linens sleep in a 'lovely linen' French dressing table. I have Foxtel, Stan, Netflix, Apple TV and YouTube, and man snacks in the pantry.

It's pleasure and pain in equal measure having Hugo in my apartment: like having a loving, mercurial, moody best friend. It takes two minutes to walk the 100 metres to his apartment (five in a sky-high heel!) and he's smart enough to know that living together wouldn't make us stronger and, if tested, it could actually make us weaker. There's something freeing about love when you have somewhere else to go!

Holidays, however, are a completely different matter. My need for a room to call my own came strongly in Italy. When I booked a *grande* suite at the Hotel Grande, I ensured there were two bathrooms: there was no way I could share a bathroom and, besides, Hugo hadn't seen me wet and naked and I wasn't about to start that caper in Italy. I couldn't go to the toilet if Hugo was in the same building, let alone the same hotel room.

I would flee to the solitude of my bathroom whenever I craved alone time or felt plain, sweaty or bloated. A woman's hair is the first thing to go mad when we're travelling, and my hair went bonkers. It was never limper, thinner or so remarkably *un*shiny than in Italy. I'd brought a set of heated hair rollers to help, which was a real drag. They took up half my suitcase and the European converter was the size of a shoe.

It wasn't that I was horribly vain or thought I was a movie star. I stared into my hand mirror and redid my thin hairdo in order to find myself again. Sometimes, I'd run a bath and lie in the suds wearing a frock, just basking in my own solitary solitude.

I'm 100 per cent confident that, upon reading this, you're now fully convinced of the advantages of the LAT lifestyle. So imagine my surprise when only a few weeks ago I was asked to turn from a LAT into a CUD. Overnight!

Hugo suggested that after ten years of Living Apart Together, we should forget *all* about that and become a couple who Cohabited Under Duress.

I was startled. This was brand new. Was it a test? A joke? Sunstroke, heatstroke and manstroke all came to mind. Hugo appeared to have immersed himself in an imaginary Living in Sin world, where he was talking earnestly about retiring to the country with goats, beehives, two studios and a fire plan.

I asked if he was under some kind of gypsy spell but he shook his head, grabbed my trembling hand and we drove to the hills to places like Sherbrooke and Olinda to 'house-kick'. We'd both fantasised about living in the country, but not until we were pensioners and Edward had left home (which was never going to happen, so I thought I was safe!).

We'd house-kicked in Olinda before, and Wye River and Italy, but this was different. He seemed determined to live as a CUD and I went along with it, if only to put my emotional need for solitude to the test. We house-kicked a gorgeous Edwardian mini-mansion and looked into purchasing a four-star hotel called the Mill with four garages and two studios with a kiln! It was good fun to taste the joys of finding a house in the hills, but I wasn't serious about the goats, the beehives or the fire plan. I was living a fantasy and it wasn't even my own. My nose was twitching – I was worrying about the every-day-sock vibe already. My neurons were in freefall, on the hunt for a honking sock.

I tried to put him off with bushfire panic. I showed Jack the dog and Hugo how to remove dead leaves from gutters while yelling modern-day fire slogans like 'get down low and go, go, go', but I almost choked on my dim sim when Hugo said he was going to become a volunteer firefighter.

Solitude gives us the time to save and preserve all our little embers of creativity, and those tiny little sparks can kickstart the greatest fire of all, the one within you!

What makes a relationship work as a LAT is trust, respect and the understanding that you're complex and might be easily irritated. Hugo and I live separately but together because if we didn't, I could be dead! Asphyxiated by the ordinariness of the everyday smells!

Not all shipwrecks are physical; there are things that can swallow up what's inside of us as easily as the sea. We all have the capacity to hide in the shadows of life, our self-made illusions and well-hidden secrets often disempowering and isolating us. We need to bring our issues into the light. To quit tying ourselves up in knots. There's something powerful about light and the way it scatters and diminishes …

I was worried I'd end up hiding in a cupboard if we Cohabited Under Duress. My olfactory bulb was flashing overtime: his screen-saver was a fire truck and seven firefighters. I had to step this up.

The week after we house-kicked, I interrupted his personal space four times and left the fridge door open many more. I didn't jump up to greet him when he came over to cook dinner, and when he anxiously played me his new album, I told him it was too loud. I lingered near his phone and asked too many questions about something that had nothing to do with me. I deliberately got a cold and then came down with a mystery illness.

I coughed all night and acted hurt and bruised when he wouldn't kiss me on the mouth. I huffed and puffed until I blew the house down!

And just like that, he came to his senses.

Of course, he's still close by; he's just around the corner. I might walk over there now. And if he's in one of his lingering, dark, creative moods, I can just leave! There's a lot of freedom in knowing when to come and when to go, when to stay and when to leave.

You can't go back and change the beginning, but you can start where you are and change the ending. In the hour we are most alone, all the love in the world is not enough, and the sight of those honking socks could finish you off.

Look out for your little room, the one you can call your own. It will keep you safe for eternity.

The shawl of *fakery*

Fakery?

It rhymes so well with bakery … and yet fakery has nothing to do with bakeries.

Fakery can be many things to many people, but the bakery of *fakery* alludes to a grim little charade, a plastic veneer, a fraud, a hypocrisy, a deliberate deception, a farce, a mockery, a travesty, or, my personal favourite, a *cover*-up!

When I was younger, I flipped fakery on its head and turned it into a cover-up. The Hobart art world talked about it for weeks, my name associated with exaggerated words like mockery, deception, troublemaking, muckraking, fakery and fraud.

Fraud?

All I did was make a raging arty mistake, and if beauty apps and selfies had been invented in 1979, I wouldn't have *had* to go into hiding for a week, accused of ruining an artist's career.

When did you last take a selfie? Yesterday? Today? Last week? Never? Ever?

I've just snapped five and it's only 11 am! I snap selfies to ensure my eyebrows aren't crooked and that my face powder is 'dewy' and not 'gluey'! I delete my mid morn *maquillage** snaps because if I didn't my I phone would be choked with selfies.

My friend Google told me that our phones are snapping ninety-four million photographs a day, with every third a selfie. Some psychologists have given selfie addicts a condition: acute selficitis! It's a mental disorder of pandemic proportions, linked to monumental levels of anxiety, depression, narcissism, loneliness, fakery, distortion and envy. People snapping endless selfies do so because they don't feel real. And a selfie proves that they are. It's like looking into a mirror, *snap snap snap*!

And if you're not already attuned to the fact, a beauty app makes you look younger, taller, thinner and sexier. You simply download it onto your phone, run your selfies through its filters, and – voila! There are thousands of different beauty apps available and the more money you spend, the more likely you are to look like a *completely* different person!

The beauty app reinvents every image taken by deceiving the world (and yourself) into believing that you're twenty years younger, with huge, innocent eyes and voluminous bee-stung lips. Your cheekbones are as high as a teenager on a Saturday afternoon, and your eyebrows? Elizabeth Taylorish! You can reshape the nose you've always disliked into a tiny little button called the 'Audrey Hepburn nose'. Your skin is Photoshop perfect. The beauty app has the power to make wrinkles, freckles, warts, pimples, sores and age spots completely disappear.

---

* *Maquillage* is French for make-up!

It's dangerous morphing your real self into a completely different person because you begin to view yourself through the lying rose-coloured glasses of the beauty app. I got a real shock last week when I brushed past a mirror in a chemist. The mirror didn't have a beauty app and seeing myself beauty-app-less came as a nasty shock. I didn't recognise the shorter, weary and more pinched version of myself!

Deep down we all think we're a little plain. (I don't know anybody who doesn't unless they're faking it!)

We squirm with uncomfortable vanity when a friend uploads images from the birthday party you both attended last week. The birthday party where you ate the wrong bread and looked eight months pregnant. The birthday party where your hair fell flat in your beetroot-red face. Your friend performed magic with her latest beauty app (on *her* but not on *you*) and she looks like a beautiful, veneered plastic version of herself, three inches taller and as thin as a reed. You're slumped beside her, more bloated than a dead body in stormy waters. You've got a double chin and you look like a pretty little pig.

Most women feel like a pretty little pig when friends upload unfiltered, unflattering images onto social media. The power abused, and trust refused, is like a 'bad reputation' – once you have a bad reputation, you're stuck with it for life. They follow you everywhere, those unbecoming, unfiltered images splashed all over the internet.

A beauty app was the last unthinkable thing on my mind when I was a young girl swanking around Hobart's Salamanca market. (Regrettably, so was ruining an artist's career. I had no idea I was only days away from accomplishing any kind of ruination!)

I'd swank through the market looking for treasures in a mini-skirt made from frozen autumn leaves and bright yellow floor paint. I teamed the autumn leaves with a blush-pink cashmere cardigan and a navy-blue wool beret with bells sewn on it, pearl necklaces and a black beauty spot on each of my rouged cheeks.

The beret's garish pompoms had little bells inside, so you could hear me coming for miles. I'd also sewed plaits onto the beret to make it appear as though I had naturally long hair. I didn't have naturally long hair. In fact, I had the worst hair in Hobart.

I had one arty friend, a political punk way ahead of his political time, the lead singer in his own band, who even wrote romantic poetry and one play called 'The Play'. Antonio wore a homemade badge made out of newspaper that said Fuck Off. He sold them at the Salamanca market for twenty cents an eff off.

I was dying to have one of those badges to wear on my lace Peter Pan collar.

Antonio's mother, who helped sell the eff-off badges, seemed inspired, intrigued and almost thrilled with my get-up. 'Are you not a sight to see?' she asked with a painterly glint in her eye as she clucked her tongue. I never knew how to respond when I was given a compliment as a question, so I'd usually serve the compliment back as a question.

'Am I a sight to see, really?'

(I think it was my way of fishing for a double compliment.)

'Yes, you are a sight to see. I studied expressionist painting in Paris ... Would you like to sit for a portrait?'

Antonio told me the family had a proper artist's studio inside their house. Did I really hear his mother correctly? Did Mrs Martino just ask if she could paint me?

Paint me?! I looked down at my latest fashion creation and wondered if Antonio's mother had seen the real expressive me. And yet, on that sunny, arty morning at Salamanca market, I agreed to something I shouldn't have – I agreed to sit for a painter. I only agreed because I thought expressionist painters were inspired by a person's expression, so I pulled some expressions to show Mrs Martino she wouldn't regret it. I did shock, sadness and fake happiness. I'd recently learnt to cry on cue, so I added that in for good measure.

My expressions must have worked because in less than five minutes it was all arranged. Mrs Martino gave me the address to her studio and told me there was a good chance I'd have to stay the night in a spare room. I understood immediately. Expressionist portraits take a long time to paint, and I figured my baroque-style make-up would make the painting time even longer.

The bus pulled into Mrs Martino's street soon after, and like little Orphan Lannie I banged on the door with my pompom head belling. Mrs Martino greeted me in a patchwork shawl. Apparently, she never took the shawl off. She loved a shawl. She was what one might call a 'shawl wearer'.

She was like a Modigliani painting come to life. Her face was long and mournful. One eye was blue and I swear the other was pale green. She wore dark-rimmed glasses across a large Italian nose and her lips were coloured in with a matte plum lipstick. Long, grey hair fell across her face in an unexpected manner. There was a steadiness to her, like all the storms in the world had passed her by.

I complimented Mrs Martino on the smells emancipating from the kitchen and she quickly corrected me – 'Emanating from the kitchen, dear, not emancipating.'

Between mouthfuls of homemade lasagne (delicious after my diet of chips and Chiko Rolls) Mrs Martino described her upcoming art show. Her biggest problem, she said, was that she'd had no inspiration for her last painting – until she met me! She told me she was experimenting with light and shade, the mystery of colour and the intrigue of texture, the subtlety of profiles and the expansion of expressionism in young girls' eyes.

Preparing to be painted and hung in a gallery, I did exactly what was asked. I sat stiller than Ben Stiller and more trustworthily than a church mouse. I wasn't permitted to move or speak because it changed my pose, so I kept my eyes open wide and did nothing but blink. I hoped I conveyed an expressive expression for Mrs Martino's experiment with light and shade, intrigue and texture. I imagined her long, skilful fingers whipping up a photographic likeness of me not dissimilar to the Mona Lisa. I mean, she was Italian and I'd spotted a book on the polished Huon pine dining table entitled *Mona Lisa: The Myth*.

The painting session was conducted in dead silence, which made me very nervous. I like people who begin by blurting out something overly personal and then go on to deliver something even more personal. I like people who tell me secrets. People with a handkerchief of bravado or a frock of triumph.

Mrs Martino seemed incapable of the kind of nattering I yearned for – faults in the family history, a murder, an illegitimate child, a cross-dressing teen or the ruination of an entire family by a scandalous sex scandal – so instead I just watched, hoping I was inspiring Mona Lisa–like expressions.

Mrs Martino artfully darted around the studio mixing colours and chemicals, and in breaks I ate marzipan for the first and last time.

After sitting dead-mannequin still for what seemed like days, Mrs Martino finally did the big reveal. There was no *tat tat tat arrrrrrr*, no balloons, no confetti, not even a photographer to catch the electrifying moment.

I slipped around to view the masterpiece. Mrs Martino moved to one side to allow me to see the full portrait horror. It was the most menacing, monstrous and grotesque thing I'd ever seen!

I didn't look like a thing like the Moaning Lisa. I looked like Moaning Alannah.

My face wasn't painterly and old-fashioned like the Mona Lisa's – Mrs Martino had painted me as a rectangle, the outline of my head a half-triangle. My face was a splintered plane of angular shards of paint with only my lips recognisable. And they were not painted red. They were twisted like twinned snakes and my nose was just two black holes.

Mrs Martino told me how she saw me in the abstract, as boxes and circles. 'The outline of you is there but you're hiding, hiding in circles – in the abstract.'

I didn't give a flying square about squared circles. I wanted to say, 'At the VERY least I hoped for a version of the Mona Lisa! You won't win an Archibald with your paint strokes. You can't paint, and I look nothing like Mona!'

Now, I've always loved to meddle in the arts with highfalutin collaborations … but this time I had to really meddle in the arts. And I had to meddle fast, before that abomination of me was found hanging in an art gallery at the Salamanca Market.

When Mrs Martino said she needed me in the morning for 'touch ups' and that I should make myself comfortable in the guest room, I planned a Radical Art move.

I waited until the house went quiet.

Dead-calm quiet.

I rolled from my mattress on the floor and wrapped myself up in an orange chenille dressing-gown that hung from a rusty nail behind the door. Barefoot, I crept down the hallway with real purpose and poise, willing myself to become invisible and very, very small, convincing myself I was doing Mrs Martino a massive favour that would save her career.

I found the grotesque painting resting on an easel, covered in a white sheet, the studio illuminated by midnight moonlight. I don't think that portrait had any idea how it was about to be changed and reborn. I chose my favourite colours, took a deep breath and began the reinvention I knew the painting needed. I had to work quickly. The sun was coming up and I'd never used paints before.

I started with my lips and painted a big red smile. I turned one of the circles into my head and the triangle into my face.

I painted black hair onto the circle and added a bright-red bow and matching pansy flower. The bow was slightly crooked, so I painted on a separate one. In cat-burglar silence, I painted thicker eyebrows, but the paint dried too quickly and began to flake. My retouched freckles resembled large moths, so I changed the moths to bows. I had no idea what I was doing but, to my credit, by the time I was finished there was no trace of Mrs Martino's original horror.

Staring back at my unrecognisable self, I suddenly felt nervous. Clutching my chenille dressing gown to my paint-spattered chest, I crept back up the hallway to the spare room, redid my make-up and waited on the edge of the bed. After applying my fifth layer of lip gloss, I heard a scream.

Sharp, quick, berserk footsteps were running toward the spare room.

'Why, Alaaaaarnaaaaaargh? Why?' Mrs Martino cried, her shawl trembling with the despair of a true artist. I was speechless, temporarily incapacitated, paralysed from the toes up, unable to comprehend why I wasn't being congratulated on my artistic breakthrough. I stood as gormless and guilty as a puppy who'd just eaten a Prada heel.

I explained in detail exactly what I had done. Her mouth opened and shut and she blinked every time I said, 'I painted over that.'

Her face was falling faster than a corpse wearing cement boots. My meddling in the arts was not appreciated here.

As I left the house, I gave the portrait one more look and noted that my eyebrows had taken a turn for the worse. The paint had dribbled onto what I'd turned into my big smile and it looked like something brown was coming out of my mouth.

I shredded the atmosphere and ran faster than Banksy with a beauty app. I didn't look left, I didn't look right and I didn't look back; I went into hiding for a week.

In those faraway golden days I was living in one room with my sister. I was upset because we were both in the process of trying to kill each other, and Mrs Martino's expressionist painting had only made it worse. I'd wanted a 1970s Facetuned selfie to make me feel beautiful … a painting to show my mum and nan to prove that I was important enough to be asked to sit for a painting. I'd seriously thought my reinvention of Mrs Martino's attempts at expression would help her flourishing career!

Since my younger art-fooled days I've sat for the Archibald Prize three times! I didn't like any of the portraits because I didn't look anything like the Mona Lisa. But did I break into the artists' studios to reinvent their paintings with a shredder and perform another Alannsky?

No, of course I didn't, because I'm more woke than a yoke, I'm more awake than a snake, and beauty doesn't live in a beauty-app filter (trust me, loves, I've searched high and low!). The beautifully sad thing about beauty is that when we look back at photographs of our younger selves we can see just how gorgeous we were with our glowing, dewy skin and pert, high breasts. Instead of feeling gorgeous we focused on all the lies we told ourselves. Never truer was the saying, 'Beauty and youth is wasted on the young.'

But, dear reader, perhaps feeling beautiful is a little like happiness – it's hard to find and, when we feel it, it only lasts ten minutes. 'Ten minutes?!' I hear you scream. 'That's not enough! Ten minutes? You've lost your marbles, Alannah! Ten minutes! Come ON!'

Of course, ten minutes isn't enough, loves, but like we do with our Handbag of Happiness, we make the perfect ten minutes worth living for, and the hours that circle them worth fighting for.

Postscript: I'm all for the art of 'faking it', but investing in a beauty app is almost forgery; we look nothing like our real selves. We're all disillusioned with the way we look, but a beauty app isn't the cure for beauty blues. Take a selfie and repeat after me … Imperfection is beauty, madness is genius and it's better to be absolutely ridiculous than absolutely boring.

Snap snap snap!

One last postscript

I've always found it hard to say goodbye, and even anguish over a fond farewell …

But because it's my last postscript, I wanted you to know that I'm ever so grateful that you took the time to read my words. I wrote *The Handbag of Happiness* in my apartment (in between holding Ed tight to my apron strings and cleaning out the fridge).

I'm sitting in the sunroom. Edward has left the front door open and the autumn chill of April has found its way inside. It's 5 pm and the birds have stopped their summer singing – the shriek of cicadas has taken their place. Falling leaves bid farewell to summer branches: leaves of brilliant yellow, wild scarlet and a sunset pink. It's quite beautiful watching autumn leaves falling while eating a violet crumble bar, and snapping a quick selfie wearing my new 'steezy' pair of Shox Nike runners! (Savers superstore in Moorabbin!)

Edward did travel to Tokyo on his playdate with three chums and had a life-changing time. I telephoned him every day and when he forgot to telephone back, I'd have a crushing, lingering nervy b, followed by a tension headache and an insane urge to call every hospital in Japan.

I'm not sure if Edward will ever get to see me sitting atop a mountain goat (wearing a ball gown) in Nepal or throw his insides up on a Himalayan beach, because of one big word: coronavirus.

Unfortunately, coronavirus and destiny told him he wasn't meant to go. (And I couldn't be happier cutting up his fruit and hand-delivering it on a Royal Doulton plate! Well, I could be happier but, like I've always said, we're mothers forever.)

Hugo and I continue to live as LATs – and due to my kindness and understanding nature, he has his own a sock and shoe drawer in my over-styled girlie apartment!

Jack, unfortunately, has been diagnosed with dog dementia, and doesn't appear to hear my shrieks whenever I call 'Jaaaaaackkkkk!' The vet implied Jack is going deaf. And blind. And, oddly enough, that he's two kilograms overweight! He sleeps on my bed on a pale-blue warming blanket and shakes with excitement when he hears my keys at the front door. (Dogs are excellent like this. At least someone is delighted to see you when you arrive home!)

A fond farewell for now, dear reader. Be strong within yourself, and when you feel like you're falling apart or dodging bullets you didn't know were being fired at you, pop on your blessing gown of silent sadness, slip on your sky-high heel of utopia, and know that you're not alone.

love, Hannah

A heartwarming thank you to ...

Hugo Race – my LAT love and confidante. Thank you for your earnest wisdom and steady flow of advice. For your ideas and being in my corner despite all my hidden vices! Thank you for delving into my handbag with me, and keeping me spinning from here to eternity!

Andrea McNamara – for whipping me into shape and encouraging me to get the 'correct' words on the page. For your shrink-like ways and concerned, supportive gaze, for helping me structure *The Handbag of Happiness* and for explaining over and over and over again what the hell 'boundaries' are!

To my publisher, Hardie Grant. And a great big giant heart-warming thank you to Arwen Summers and Loran McDougall, for once again allowing me to edit over and over and over again!

And to Edward, my son, the love of my life.

Published in 2020 by Hardie Grant Books,
an imprint of Hardie Grant Publishing

Hardie Grant Books (Melbourne)
Building 1, 658 Church Street
Richmond, Victoria 3121

Hardie Grant Books (London)
5th & 6th Floors
52–54 Southwark Street
London SE1 1UN
hardiegrantbooks.com

A catalogue record for this
book is available from the
NATIONAL
LIBRARY   National Library of Australia
OF AUSTRALIA

The Handbag of Happiness
ISBN 978 1 74379 633 7

10 9 8 7 6 5 4 3 2 1

Publisher and Copyeditor: Arwen Summers
Project Editor: Loran McDougall
Developmental Editor: Andrea McNamara
Design Manager: Jessica Lowe/Mietta Yans
Designer: Murray Batten
Production Manager: Todd Rechner

Colour reproduction by Splitting Image Colour Studio
Printed in China by Leo Paper Products LTD.

The paper this book is printed on is from FSC®-certified forests and other sources.
FSC® promotes environmentally responsible, socially beneficial and
economically viable management of the world's forests.